My Sisters and Me

By Margaret Lewis-Wilbur
Illustrations by Sarah Denbigh

Order this book online at www.trafford.com
or email orders@trafford.com

Most Trafford titles are also available at major online book retailers.

Print information available on the last page.

ISBN: 978-1-4120-9484-9 (sc)
ISBN: 978-1-4251-9516-8 (e)

Trafford rev. 06/17/2021

Trafford
PUBLISHING®   www.trafford.com
North America & international
toll-free: 844-688-6899 (USA & Canada)
fax: 812 355 4082

Dedication

I wish to thank a number of people who helped me tremendously and encouraged me to create this book, namely Karen Lewis, my children Rhonda, Brian, Kathy and David and their families and my husband Harley.

Introduction

I was born at a time when my people loved nature and spoke of it as though it had a soul. I was always surrounded by laughter and smiling faces of my people. I felt very much loved and protected; we sang, danced and heard wonderful stories. I didn't know it then but by telling these stories was their way of teaching. I had some wonderful teachers, very understanding people all of whom were family members who knew the importance of our ways of life and what was expected of each and every one of us. We were expected to pass on our knowledge to the next generation; this is what I've been trying to do. These stories always made me happy and important lessons were being taught. I didn't know what was happening then but in later years I understood how important all those teachings were. This book contains some of my experiences growing up on Tyendinaga Reserve, a Mohawk community on the Bay of Quinte in Ontario.

Tyendinaga

TYENDINAGA IS MY HOME TERRITORY WHICH is located on the Bay of Quinte in Ontario about forty miles West of Kingston on number two highway where I spent all my growing, learning, sharing, loving times with my whole family.

I remember playing in the water at the Bay Of Quinte, 'the Beach'. We lived there for ever it seemed but my grandmother Chic whose name was really Margaret Ellen, lived at a place called Point Anne with my two uncles. I remember the first time I saw Point Anne it was on a clear warm day and mom was with us kids at the beach and she said to me,

"Do you see that big chimney way across the bay?"

I said "Yes."

"Well that's where Chic lives."

"How is she going to come over here and see us?" I asked.

Mom said "Wait and see, she has a surprise way of getting here. Just be patient, wait and see."

"I get lonesome for Chic." I told mom.

Mom went home and I stayed at the bay and played for a while. I had my dog and my little birch bark canoe. I remember squatting down at the edge of the water then getting up really quick looking towards Point Anne in the direction of the big chimney. When I looked a little more closely I thought I saw someone way out on the bay. I thought it might be Jakey out fishing. I waited until they got closer and saw it was Chic. I could see my two uncles with my grandmother Chic, this is what I called her and she would only laugh when I called her that; they would be coming from Point Anne in a big row boat to see us. When they were quite a ways out Chic would stand up in the boat and wave the oars which mom told me indicated they had fish. Then I would run up to the house and tell mom and we would all go back down to the beach to meet them. My dad always made a big fire because we would stay there for supper. All the neighbours came down and joined us; they brought food also and we shared what we had with each other.

All the children would be going up and down the shore looking for firewood. We found enough wood to cook our supper. We all enjoyed a good meal of fry bread, corn soup and fish. After we finished eating we all washed our tin plates in the water and scrubbed them with sand then laid them on some long grass and rocks to dry. After supper my dad and some other people would play their fiddles and other instruments. My pappadad would play the spoons and everyone would be dancing, laughing even the children; I always liked to step dance whenever I heard fiddle music. Nearly everyone I knew could play some sort of instrument. The dance floor was a door from Oliver Hill's barn. We all had a wonderful time. We all seemed happy. This was our way to cope with all the stress brought on by the Indian agent. This kept us going. The most important thing was we were all together, that's how we survived. I'll always remember these times; they were very dear and important in my life and still are.

Tale Of A Horse Tail

AUNT EMMA WAS MY FATHER'S OLDEST SISTER and we called her aunt Bobbi. She never lived with us at the beach because she was away working as a milliner in the big city. She came home one time to visit us and brought a surprise for dad.

"What is it?"

She handed dad a little brown bag and told him to open it. To his surprise it was horse hair for his fiddle bow. Dad thanked her and said,

"There's enough here for fifty years. Where did you get it?"

She said, "I took the bus and it stopped along the road to let the people get out and stretch their legs. While outside the bus I noticed a grey horse standing by the fence. In my hand I had an apple and pair of long scissors from my purse. I gave the horse the apple and while he was eating it I cut off his tail. Here it is, I give it to you because I always knew you needed some hair for your fiddle bow."

Everyone sat down and laughed so hard they were crying. Dad said,

"Now some farmer has a horse with no tail and he's trying to find out what happened."

Papadad wanted to know,

"What was the horse going to do to shoo the flies away?"

The more they talked about this the harder everyone laughed. Aunt Bobbi wanted to know,

"What must you do to the horse hair to prepare it so it could be used for your bow?"

Dad told her "Mom would wash it to get it good and clean then it had to be left to dry for quite a while."

Mom said "I'll take it down to the beach and beat it against some rocks."

She did wash the horse hair for dad and hung it on the line to dry inside an old ladies sock.

After the hair was dry dad and mom took it one strand at a time and laid each one in opposite direction. The reason for this is the hair has barbs on them and that's the way you attach them to the bow. This is what makes the sound when you draw the bow over the strings. I watched them do this and dad even counted them because you need to be this precise. It took them a long time. Papadad said,

"If you don't hurry up I'll be too old to play the fiddle."

It took mom and dad a long time to put the hair in the right places. The time had come for aunt Bobbi to leave us again. We were all sad to see her go, I asked her,

"Where are you going?"

"To Chicago." she answered.

I had no idea where this place was, as far as I knew it could have been to the end of the world. I was just repeating what my mom said. I recalled dad telling her she didn't have to get any more horse tail. She hugged dad and she and him had a good laugh. Then she hugged and kissed each one of us. She asked dad to look after grandma and papadad, he just nodded. It came my turn, I got on a chair and hugged her, she told me,

"Keep dancing."

"I will as long as dad and papadad keep playing the fiddle."

We never said goodbye we always said on:en.

Dad walked with her up the beach road to get the bus in Shannonville. As they were walking up the road I was playing and watching them as they were going. They went out of sight and I ran back to the house to ask mom,

"How come I can't see her getting on the bus?"

Mom said "Because she and dad had to walk a different way to get to the bus."

I didn't understand what all this meant so I stopped asking questions.

"Can I go and meet dad?"

"No, we will all go and meet dad."

I ran out to the road and saw someone coming a long ways away; it turned out to be Peter 'Boots' Williams. It took a long time then I saw someone else coming. I ran back to the house and told mom,

"Let's go see who it is, it must be dad because he's been gone for a long time. Its dad, I can tell by the way he's walking."

I ran up the road and was the first to reach him.

"Dad, it's nice to see you."

He picked me up, "It's nice to see you too."

"Did aunt Bobbi get the bus okay?"

He said, "Yes, she asked me to give you this."

It was a black licorice pipe. I didn't know it was candy and told papadad,

"I have a pipe like the one you have."

"Where did you get it?"

"Aunt Bobbi told dad to give it to me."

"Now we can smoke our pipes together when we go for a walk. Did you put it in your mouth yet? Does it taste good?"

"It has fire on it but there is no smoke." I said.

"That's a funny pipe, maybe you should eat it."

Mom told papadad, "She has sweet black lips."

I don't remember what happened to my pipe I must have eaten it but papadad had his for ever.

Skating On The Bay

THE WINTER WAS SOMETIME BEFORE MY papadad traded places and we all went down to the bay to play on a large piece of ice that my dad and other men had kept free of drifting snow. The plow they used was made of two boards fastened in a vee with two handles going back from it so two men could push and also had a rope to be used to pull it by some other men in front. They had cleaned off several spots, one for the kids, one for older people to play shinny and one for just skating. The snow that was pushed back from the ice made a bank and a place for us to sit. We never had skates and just used our sleigh to slide around on; we really had a lot of fun. There was one time aunt Phyllis put her skates on me and took me down to the bay on the sleigh and stood me there on the ice. I was about seven. She stuffed some socks in the toes to fill up the space. I looked around very carefully and didn't move an inch, I was so scared then along came dad who took me by both hands and skated with me between his legs. I'll tell you I never moved an inch I was so stiff. Dad told me to relax; I didn't know what he meant so I just held on for dear life. We must have spent the better part of the day there because I was some tired when I got home. Mom had our night time meal ready for us and I was so tired I conked out before I ate. The next day we did the same thing all over again and I was still scared. It must have taken the better part of the winter for me to get up enough courage to try to move my feet and what a struggle it was. I recall trying so hard to walk in my snow shoes that dad and papadad had made but the skates were a lot different because my feet were sliding sideways and front wards and I couldn't walk in them either no matter how hard I tried. Some time during the night we got an awful lot of snow and dad told mom it wasn't really cold out so he was going down to the bay to clean off the ice. He wasn't gone long and when he returned he told mom the snow was too heavy and he couldn't do it all. Uncle Oliver hitched up his team of horses and went down to the bay and cleaned off the rink. Everyone was pleased; there seemed to be as many people gathered in the winter as there was in the summer, we even had a lot of fun having sleigh rides, falling off the sleigh and running to catch it. Mom had a jug of hot apple cider when we were down at the beach and when she gave us a drink we seemed to have more energy and didn't want to go home. As I look back there wasn't much to do for the older people in the winter which became some of the special times they spent with the children. Later when we were at home it would be story telling time.

One evening after we had eaten our night time meal we heard some people talking and laughing; we looked out our window and along the shore there was quite a pile of snow where dad saw lights moving along the bank. Dad lit the lantern and decided to go and have a look, when we got to the bay we saw it was the Green family and that's all it took for other people to show up soon after. I remember looking up in the sky and Grandmother Moon was really fat. I told mom she was smiling at us and mom just smiled at me and nodded. I asked mom how come she was up and mom said we were having so much fun she decided to join us for a while. When I looked down at the snow it was all sparkly like trillions of diamonds, it was a magnificent sight for a little girl to cherish and remember. The men had all their lighted lanterns sitting on top of the piled up snow and between the moon and the lantern light it was almost like day time. I could even see Point Anne where Chic lived. Everyone didn't have skates so aunt Phyllis finally took mine off so I could play with the rest of the children; we had a lot fun when I lived there.

I hadn't noticed that dad had a fire on the shore. He had dug a hole in the snow and piled some rocks high inside the hole beside an old willow tree. It took some time to get the fire going , dad and some other men had brought some wood from home so it would be easier to start the fire and keep it going. I asked dad if we were going to fry some fish and he said yes. Pete Williams dug a hole in the ice way out in the bay and got enough fish for everybody. Mom brought some fry bread from home, what a wonderful feast we had. Dad had his fiddle; mom stood on the bank and said she would call for a square dance if anybody is willing to dance. It was the funniest thing we had ever seen, if you could picture all these people trying to square dance on the ice, there were more people down than there were standing. I think about how hard everyone worked and how they all worked together to keep our traditions alive and to pass them on. It turned out it was a midwinter ceremony. I remember dad saying it had something to do with Grandmother Moon and what the rest of our winter was going to be like and how important it was to always remember. I can't recall too much about the specifics of the ceremony but some I do. Community togetherness, births of that year and our family members who had traded places. The fire was always the centre of our lives where we did our singing and dancing. These times in my life were very important to me; I relive a lot of them. We as Mohawk people have something so special and unique as a nation that I won't let it go. I know in my heart that my family taught these things for a reason to keep our culture alive and I know they intended for me to share these stories of events with my people at Tyendinaga.

Pig's Head

I DON'T KNOW WHO THE PEOPLE were but someone had given mom a pigs head along with other parts of the pig. The three of us didn't know that any of this had happened. That night after we went to bed mom sat the pigs head on a plate in the middle of the kitchen table. Dad always left the lamp lit on low so we could find our way around when we got up. Sometime in the middle of the night Carmel went down stairs to the washroom and had to pass through the kitchen on her way; that is when we heard her start screaming. She woke all of us and we wondered what had happened and we all came downstairs and there she stood too frightened to tell us what occurred. After she calmed down a bit she told mom,

"The devil is in the kitchen on the table."

The pig's eyes were open and glazed over and the light from the lamp was shining in the them. When Barb and I came downstairs we went straight to the kitchen neither one of us knew what it was either and it really did look scary. We clung to each other screaming right along with Carmel. After mom and dad managed to calm us down except Carmel who took a little longer, we never did go back to bed but stayed up for the rest of the day.

Sometime during the next day mom and Chic cooked the pigs head to make head cheese. I never cared for this kind of food and never ate any. I asked mom,

"Is this all that's left of the pig that you and grandma Rose cooked one day when I went all over looking for pigs that had no feet?"

Mom said, "No, that was a long time ago and this is a different pig."

Chic lived in the other side of the house and mom's sister and her son lived with her. They told mom,"We heard the commotion and wondered what had happened."

Mom began to explain. Aunt Phoebe asked Carmel,

"What did it look like?"

She said, "It had eyes that looked like a fish just staring at me and its mouth was all puckered up like this."

"And you didn't know what it was?"

"No, I thought it was the devil."

"Do you know what the devil looks like?"

"Just like the pigs head."

Everyone was laughing after that but Carmel didn't think it was funny.

It didn't really seem to matter where we were living something always happened that wasn't funny at the time. As we grew up and look back it was funny and we did have a lot of fun. My two sisters and I recall this episode and laugh all over again. We didn't know why mom had just left it there, she probably never thought it would scare us especially Carmel.

Playing With A Weasel

DAD WAS HELPING A NEIGHBOUR PITCHING hay and Barb and I were given the job of delivering drinking water to the field where he was working; mom gave us a honey pail full to take to him. We took a little detour to the area where some people had chipped in and removed some rocks from the field and piled them up in the corner of the fence where a big elm tree stood. We sat the water beside some rocks in the shade and as we sat there we were picking little flowers, making bouquets and placing them in the button holes on our dresses. Just then we thought we had seen something moving but we weren't sure until it happened again. We both just looked at it; we saw a small animal looking at us from between the rocks. It had a small head, tiny ears and little round black eyes with long whiskers beside its lips; I can't remember what colour it was. It was making a clicking sound and boy was it ever quick, in a split second it was looking at us from behind another rock and when it moved it went so fast we didn't see its feet. We thought it was playing hide and seek with us; it would hide and we would go looking for it and it never came out where we were looking. We were lying on our bellies; we had scraped our knees and elbows and had a lot of grass stains on our dresses.

We were so taken in by this little animal that we hadn't noticed dad walking on the path that led along the edge of the bush with a white handkerchief tied in four knots and placed on his head. We hadn't even noticed our lunch was in a pail tied on a branch in the elm tree. When he came a little closer and sat down on the rocks beside us and asked,

"What have you two been doing?"

We both started telling dad what we had seen and tried to describe it in a very excited voice. He said.

"Slow down, only one at a time." So we took turns telling him what we saw, what it looked like and how quick it was and it didn't have any feet.

"Wait until I see it and I will be able to tell you what it is. Did you bring the water?"

"Yes it's over here." I said. I got the pail of water and dad got the food from the tree.

Dad thanked Creator for our food and we asked him to join us. As we began to eat there in between some rocks he showed himself but dad missed seeing him that time; the next time he peeked at us dad saw him. Barbara and I were so excited we were stuttering asking dad "What is it?"

"Calm down and I'll tell you what it is."

He told us what it was in Mohawk and it is on'on:kote. In English it is a weasel.

While we were having lunch weasel was having fun playing with my sister and I, hopping in and out from between the rocks. We gave weasel little pieces of fry bread, he didn't eat it in front of us he ran and hid with it. Dad sat with us for a while before he went back pitching hay and he left the rest of the food on the ground in case Barbara and I wanted more. We gave a few more pieces of bread to weasel, we saved some to take home with us because we were not allowed to waste anything. The rest of the day was spent playing and watching weasel and running around in the hay field. We were both tired and decided to lie down on the ground and look at the clouds; we saw different kinds of animals in the cloud formations but no weasel. We had a lot of fun that day. We waited for dad to finish work so we could walk home together. Barbara was hanging on dads hand and I was hopping and jumping backwards in front of them.

Dad asked, "Are you going to tell mom how you spent the day and what you both saw?"

We both said "Yes."

We went back to the rock pile quite often after that and sometimes we were lucky enough to see weasel. These are some of the things we did when we were small and we even learned some lessons about other different animals in particular the animals we never saw before. In the winter time we were told stories by papadad about different animals and I found these stories very fascinating when told in a human way. The stories are also lessons we have learned and how we are like these animals in so many ways, they should always be respected by everyone.

Dad told us, "When winter comes this little animal turns white because he has to go out and look for food and his colour helps to protect him from being harmed."

I said "It's like magic that he can change his colour."

Dad said, "No, Creator made him like this because he isn't very big and he also has another defense namely he is very, very quick. He darts in and out of hiding places; sometimes you don't even see him; this makes it hard for other animals to catch him.

Our Well

—————➤●◄—————

ON THE NORTH SIDE OF OUR house outside the kitchen window was our well. Dad asked mom to keep us away from it because he was afraid we might fall in. It wasn't too deep but was quite wide and dad and papadad decided to dig it deeper while mom wanted a base around it for safety. Down he went with a big bucket tied to a rope and when it was full of debris papadad would hoist it up, empty it and return the bucket to dad and I'm sure this went on for days or at least that is what it seemed to me. While this was going on Joker Brant and grandpa Con kept us in drinking water and Joker and 'Jakey' Brant would come over and help dad whenever possible. As the digging was going on, uncle Oliver went to the beach with his horse and wagon to bring back certain size rocks to be used to line the well. Dad told papadad the digging was getting rather tough right now because he ran into some clay so papadad said he'd tell me to go and get a crow bar. Dad said okay but he was also digging in pockets of sand which makes good filtering system and papadad agreed. Dad and everyone else worked really hard but the benefits would be good, we would have a lot more water when the well was finished. After digging for quite a while dad decided it was deep enough and they started to place the stones around the wall and everyone took turns even Peter 'Boots'. They worked on the well from daylight to dark in all kinds of weather. The well was finally finished and dad put a top on it like mom had asked and we had a pail that hung in the well at all times. Now we had to wait until the Creator filled our well from the rain water and it did take a long time to fill our well. I was always the one to get water for mom to do the cooking and make grandma some tea; I was going to the well once every few minutes. Mom told me to go and play, I didn't need to go there so often. Papadad said I would make a good person to lasso anything; of course I wanted to know what a lasso was. Papadad said it was a long rope with a hoop at the end and when it was thrown it lands over something or someone. I wanted to know if it had a pail tied to it and he just laughed at me.

Summer was passing by and dad was going to build a higher box to cover the well which he did with papadads help. Someone had given dad a pump and now he had to see if he could find a long pipe to reach the bottom of the well and he never did any work on the well for quite some time. One day he had been pitching hay for someone and this person had a long pipe lying beside their barn so dad asked this person if he could trade a day's work for this pipe and he agreed. Mom said I could go and meet dad now and I ran in the direction of Green's house when I saw dad coming across the hay field and I ran to meet him. I asked him what was the big pipe he was dragging home for and he said he would show me when we got home so I helped carry it. When we got home dad was so tired he lay down on the floor by the stove and went to sleep. When he got up we all had our night time meal. He and papadad showed me how they were going to use the pipe and I was watching quite closely what everyone was doing and some of the neighbour men came and gave dad a hand. This all took some time and dad fought real hard to get the pipe situated in the right spot in the bottom of the well. Dad measured where to put the pipe with a stick so it was in the centre of the hole; I guess dad approved and everybody proceeded with job at hand. They finally finished before summer was over.

The other small job was to put the pump on the pipe. When this was finished I was always the one to get the water and the first one to use the pump. I grabbed hold of the handle and tried to pull it down with my hands and both my feet were up off the ground kicking in every direction because I was too little to pull the handle down. Mom was watching but wouldn't help because I was determined to pump the water; they all just stood and laughed. We had a red water pail that sat on a bench in the kitchen and I took it outside to get water in it. After I pumped it full I started to carry it back to the house holding it with both hands between my legs and papadad could hear me grunting and asked me what I was doing. I told him I was trying to get the pail of water in the house. He told me to put the pail down and come and get him so he could help me. When I got him to the pail he bent over and asked me to put his hands on its ears. I was looking around for ears and he wondered what was taking me so long, and I told him I didn't know a pail had ears. He asked me to help him sit down and I told him he was not by his stump so he said he wanted to sit right where he was on the ground. Then he told me to come to him, he was laughing so hard and hugging me and we were both laughing he told me I was a silly little girl. Mom came out by this time and wanted to know if papadad was sick and he said no but would tell her later what went on.

Having the well just outside the kitchen door made it a lot easier for everyone because now dad didn't have to go to the beach to bring water back in the wagon in our two big barrels and we were thankful. I loved living there, we had everything we ever needed for making a good living along with the love and understanding and the special relationship with all the people who lived there. We were all family. This is what's missing today and we have to regain this relationship; it would be better for everyone. As I see it things would be much better for us if we showed the world or at least our own community how we can all pull together as one people. There are so many things that we are struggling with and it should not be left up to a few individuals to speak for us. We are good people who had fun and did a lot of things as family and I'd do it all again. The whole community was considered as family.

Off Cutting Wood

I REMEMBER MY MOM AND DAD taking a job cutting wood for a person whose name I can't remember but the place where we lived was outside the village of Marlbank which is North of Napanee. I recall it was winter and very cold and the snow was quite deep. The house that we stayed at was a two story frame house quite a way in from the highway. Aunt Ina and Jack McFarlane took us there in their car. They stayed with us for a while and aunt Ina just lay on the cot with a tooth ache for a while. Dad told her if she didn't get up he was going to get some fresh cow chips and make a poultice for her tooth. After hearing this she got up right a way. The only tools that mom and dad had with them was a cross cut saw and an axe. I remember mom and dad having no winter coat, dad had on papadad's pea jacket and mom had on her brother's coat. We all wore black rubber boots with two or three pairs of socks. Dad chopped a wedge on one side then he and mom sawed through from the other side to fell the tree; after which they would limb it and cut it into four foot lengths. When they cut the log a certain length if it wasn't too big Barb and I would take hold of each end and carry it to the sleigh. When the sleigh was full the man would come back and take the load of wood to the highway and pile it beside the road. This activity lasted forever. We were allowed to keep some of the short pieces for our own use.

I was so tired I don't remember eating; I just lay on the floor beside the stove and went to sleep. We didn't have a bed; dad threw a thick tick on the floor in the same room where he and mom slept. I remember him getting up in the night and tending to the fire. They would get us up before daylight and aunt Ina would cook us a big dish of porridge and toasted fry bread. Some times she and Jack would help mom and dad. I never thought of us as being poor, I didn't know what poor was since everyone was in the same boat. Maybe that was the best way to live. I can't remember how many loads of wood we cut but we worked until dark. Before this person drove away with the last load of logs for the day he paid mom and dad for that days work. Mom and dad kept on cutting until they couldn't see any longer and Barb and I would keep piling them on the empty sleigh. When they finished for the day Mom and dad had a lantern they would light and dad would take us by the hand and we all walked home. Since aunt Ina had a tooth problem she became the cook for a few days. We ate a lot of corn soup. We all went to bed early every night. I remember Chic made some extra quilts that year and she gave us some to take with us. I asked her once if grandpa had given her a ring when he married her and she said he had and she wore it around her neck where he put it a thousand years ago. We had a good laugh. She was a very special and wonderful grandmother. Dad closed the top part of the house off because it was too hard to heat but we were allowed to go up stairs and play some times where we had a lot of fun making designs on the single pane window. We called mom to have a look at what we were doing and she said Jack Frost was playing with us. We played X's and O's and all kinds of games, we even drew animals then we would sit and laugh at how funny they looked. Mom went back down stairs and in a few minutes she called us for our night time meal.

We were not allowed to play upstairs after we ate. Dad always kept it nice and cozy downstairs. Another part of our lives that we survived and faced a lot of challenges that we managed to get through okay. We were taught about things we needed not about things we wanted.

Mom and aunt Ina and Jack went to town for groceries and while they were gone we had a really bad snow storm and bitter cold weather. Dad waited up nearly all night for them to come back and when they finally arrived he was glad to see them all safe. They told him it took about three hours to shovel snow to get in from the highway and the groceries all froze. Mom asked dad if everything was okay and dad said Margaret scared us half to death when she pulled down the green shade and let go of it and it flew up the window making a funny clacking noise and he didn't see what happened. When Jack came in he hollered who, who, who. I asked dad was it an owl and he said no it was just Jack.

Mom and dad worked hard all their lives to keep the family together as I'm sure everyone else did. We've learned how to share and care and to watch out for each other as this is the way things ought to be especially in this country. All aboriginal people must pull together as one. It is the soul of our very existence. I look back at these trying times and I have so much pride in who I am; I've never had any intention of ever being assimilated. I am very strong for the things I know and believe in; they have brought me this far. I am proud being a Mohawk woman from my home territory, Tyendinaga.

Playing With The Greens

———⟫●⟪———

WHEN WE WERE ALL LITTLE LIVING at the beach my Aunt Phoebe and her son Peter lived with us. He's a year older than Carmel and I feel as though he is my brother. Johnny and Martha Green and family lived between Point Anne and Kimberley Town on a point of land where there were a lot of big flat rocks covered with moss. We were allowed to walk along the bay shore until we reached the Green's house so we could play all afternoon with Ila and Wilma. They had three brothers and I don't really know what their real names were, one was Snooks, another was Boobs and the other was Alvin. I was told to give Mrs. Green a note from mom to let us know when to return home. Mrs. Green would make us all something to eat at lunch time; she gave us fry bread and jam. She allowed us to go to the waters edge to eat our lunch. We had great times playing all afternoon and found all sorts of water bugs. We would blow bubbles in the water with reeds we had picked.

We saw her coming towards us, she said "It's time to go home now kids, be careful and we'll see you later."

So I took Peter by the hand and Barbara had Carmel and we headed home along the shore. I asked the little ones if they had to use the toilet. Here is a two and three year old looking for the toilet. We were singing and running in and out of the water and Peter decided he had to go! I was having an awful time trying to get him to squat down and he didn't want to and he was jumping up and down crossing his legs. I told him to hold it. There were a lot of young poplar saplings growing in the area and I bent one over, took Peter's pants down, set him on the sapling and told him to hang on and Barbara was holding it down with her foot and I told her not to walk away. Everything went well. I told him not to get up until I found a mullen leaf. So we all used the toilet and even this was done in a circle. We all finished and started on our way again, we came across some big flies that were biting us. The little ones started to cry so I took them all into the water. We went the rest of the way crawling on our hands and knees until we got to the part of the beach that we were familiar with. We stood up and walked out of the water and our knees were sore from rubbing them in the sand. We all ran home and our parents asked if we had lots of fun at the Green's.

Mom said "What happened to your little knees, there all red?"

Peter said "We swimmed all the way home!"

The next time we wanted to play with the Green kids they came to our house.

People aren't able to do things like this now and have fun like we did, that's a shame. Our parents never seemed to worry about us going and playing in the water unsupervised. We seemed to have more freedom than the people have today. I travel to these special places quite often and am so pleased that I have these memories to dream about. We took our youngest daughter Kathy and her husband Ivan down to the beach one year after the powwow and showed them approximately where I grew up and gave her a special stone from the beach. I must admit it was very emotional for me but I'll go back there every chance I get and just walk around and relive all the memories.

My Dad The Orangeman

DAD WAS A LIFETIME MEMBER OF the Orange Lodge in Point Anne. He never seemed to participate in the activities of the lodge but when the twelfth of July rolled around he stood up to be counted and was quite willing to march in the parade; he was a fife player. We were living in Shannonville and dad was invited to go to Trenton to march in the parade, I believe uncle Jim Sero drove us all there. We all gathered at a park by the river where members from different communities assembled themselves preparing for the parade. Dad led the people from Point Anne and they were the first group to start the parade. Dad played his fife and just ahead of dad Barbara and I carried the banner. The pole carrying the banner was too heavy for one of us to hold so they put the harness around both Barbara and I so we could carry the banner in the pouch between us. Ahead of us was a baton twirler who would give directions where we should go. We heard the drums and fifes quite loud and I was really marching lifting my feet as high as I could.

I also remember trying to step dance and dad hollered, "No! No!"

This was quite an honour for my sister and I and I'm not

sure how far we walked but we ended up back at the park where we started from. We rested and had some drinks and something to eat. After we rested we went a different route, this time we marched through downtown Trenton and mom and Carmel were walking beside us on the sidewalk. Somehow Carmel got away from mom, she was running and playing in front of Barbara and me, and then she took off and ran into one of the stores. Mom didn't miss her for a few minutes then you could tell by the look on mom's face that she had panicked. Barb and I had to leave the parade to help find Carmel; she was gone for quite a while. Along the street which was blocked off people were pushing wracks of clothing all up and down and Carmel was running among them. We finally spotted her and took her back to where mom was. Mom was laughing and crying at the same time, I guess that meant she was glad to see everybody. Carmel had been crying a lot since her eyes were all red. Mom and Carm went back to the park and Barb and I ran up the street to catch up with dad. Dad was carrying the banner; we stopped for a few moments so dad could put the banner back on us. We marched again for a long time. We finally got back to the park where mom and Carmel were and it was hot and Barbara just lay in the grass. I was standing on the edge of the road waiting for the rest of the parade and the drums and all the music made me happy, I remember jumping around. Dad went to join mom and Carmel and Barb and I went too. Uncle Jim had bought us a thing called a hot dog; he had it in a bag.

He opened the bag and offered me one and I said "I'm not eating this dog."

Dad said, "Go ahead, its ok."

"Can I see it first?" I said.

Everyone laughed at me. Before we ate I found it quite odd that dad didn't build a fire. I asked him about it and dad said" We don't have a fire here because this is not our home, we are just visiting". Dad did give thanks to Creator for our food and for watching over us and helping find Carmel. That was quite an experience; we really did enjoy ourselves and glad to have been asked to carry the banner.

I don't ever remember going to another Orange parade but dad continued his parade activities in the lodge. As we got older and were able to be left alone, mom would accompany dad when he would go to march in a parade.

There were other wives, who would go along with their husbands, I'm glad mom was able to go. They usually had stories to tell us when they got home and sometimes even a treat. There were quite a few aboriginal people in the lodge; I'm assuming they were Mohawks. I do remember going to another parade in Picton. We stayed with dad's cousin whose name was Evelyn and Dick Beasley was her husband. When we got there it was time for lunch and we had corn soup and fry bread. We didn't visit off reserve very often because it was too much bother to get the letter. Dad would often say "Remind me to get the letter", but I didn't always because I was too young to remember. These were great and important times for us.

Making Brooms

WHEN I WAS LITTLE WE LIVED not far from the Bay of Quinte. I remember wanting to go with my dad, especially if he was going to the bush. I knew we had a good chance to see an animal or two and he would tell me all about them and I always listened carefully to what people were talking to me about. Dad and I took off for the bush; I was happy running and playing in front of him. I fell down in front of him and skinned both knees. He picked me up and asked me "Are you okay?"

"Yes." I said.

When he put me down I asked him "What are we looking for?"

He just smiled at me and said "Come on."

I remember sometimes it was medicine we were looking for or looking at our trap line. Not this time. He said. "We are looking for some small poplar saplings."

"What for?"

"I'll show you what kind and maybe you can help me find some, okay?" he said.

As I was running along in front of dad again I tripped and fell. He asked me "What is the matter with you?"

There were some old dead twigs lying on the path.

Dad asked me "Are you hurt?"

"Nope, just got wet."

He stopped while I picked myself up and we continued on our way. We walked for quite a while.

I told dad "We were just walking around in a great big circle."

He asked me "Do you remember being here before?"

"No, the bush looks different. Where are we dad?"

"Just down behind Uncle Oliver's house, now do you know where you are?"

I said "No, 'cause I can't see Uncle Oliver's barn."

Dad said "It's away over that way towards the bay."

I said "Okay."

We walked around there for some time because whatever dad was looking for it had to be perfect. We had left our wagon at the edge of the bush.

Finally dad said "Here we are."

"Okay." I said.

Dad had a little saw he called a buck saw. He measured the trees between thumb and finger, that way he could remember he had the right size. Then he cut them off about six inches from the ground. After we had cut a bunch of these little trees we got down on our knees, he held my hand; we lifted up our heads and talked to Creator,

"You know my little girl, I'm teaching her all these ceremonies and why we have to do them so she will know how to use them when she grows up."

Then he said to me "These lessons are important. When you take from Mother Earth never pull things up by the root, if you do, none of those things will ever grow again, and that's why I cut the trees close to Mother Earth. Do you understand?"

I said "Yes."

We were there for a long time because dad took a knife and scraped all the bark from the young trees. When he had finished that again we knelt down on Mother Earth and sprinkled all this bark around the same places where dad had cut the trees off.

He said "We give this back to Mother Earth so she again will let these little trees grow for our future use."

I didn't really know what this meant, but I never forgot those words. It took us three or four trips back and forth to carry all of our little trees to where the wagon was. Dad laid them in a neat pile in the wagon and tied them down with some pieces of old deer hide that were cut in strips. On our way home I was walking behind the wagon hanging onto the trees, I don't suppose I was helping but I thought I was. We got home at our night time meal. Papadad asked "How far did you go?"

Dad told him. Papadad said "That was a long ways for Dolly to walk."

Dad said "She did just fine; she was jumping and running all the way over there."

Dad asked me to tell papadad what we did. I'm sure dad was just testing my memory. In the next little while after the trees dried out a bit, Papadad had the job of making sure one end of the tree was sanded and the other end was left natural and covered with pine gum and then mom and dad placed the straw around it. Mom would intertwine string through the straw while dad was turning the broom to fasten the straw and handle together. After this mom would tightly wrap strips of cloth around the handle and down over the straw to make it more secure. Dad cut the straw off square about twenty inches from where the straw was attached to the broom handle. When the brooms were finished dad stood them all up along the house straw end up to dry. It's not important to make brooms any more but it is important that the ceremonies were done when anything was being used from Mother Earth.

This is what we as Mohawk people need to do out of love and respect for our way of life and Mother Earth. One of the most important rules in our society is to share. Our prestige doesn't come from wealth we accumulate but what we give away.

Chic's Beaded Leggings

I WAS ALWAYS INQUISITIVE AND FOREVER asking questions and of course getting into everyone's hair but no one ever got cross with me. I guess that's how come I learned so many things and I know it has paid off.

Dad made a table that mom and everyone else used from time to time. It was sitting outdoors not far from our Sacred fire that dad always had burning. I remember this quite well because mom helped dad to make corn husk brooms on this table and one of these brooms was used to keep the area clean around the fire. He taught me also how to sweep to keep this area clean. Keeping this area clean and looking after the Sacred fire was very important to my dad. He was always telling me how important this was and he kept reminding me all the time. I learned this and never forgot.

It was one hot day and Chic said to me "I'm sweating."

"What's that?" I asked her looking her right in the face and whispering.

"That's what happens when your body gets warm and that's why you're running around only in your underwear."

Chic was sitting by the table so I wandered over to see what she was doing. She showed me what she was going to do. There were two pieces of odd shaped deer hide lying on the table.

She asked me "Do you remember helping grandma to tan it?"

"Yes, it took forever."

She had kept saying to try this, do this, and now help me take it to the beach. It was so heavy we couldn't pick it up so we tugged at it until we got it on our wagon and we pulled it through the sand down to the water. I remember walking a long ways out into the water until it was deep enough to cover the wagon. Chic told me get in the wagon and jump up and down on the hide. I did and it was so slippery that I slipped and fell out of the wagon into the water. Chic grabbed me by the hair and pulled me out of the water and hanging on my hand we looked at each other and laughed so hard they could hear us all the way to Shannonville. I remember Chic shaking salt all over the hide and I had a thousand questions,

"Are we going to eat this?"

She said "No, why?"

"Because it's too hard to chew."

She took my hands and we both laughed out loud. We turned the wagon around in the water, she was pulling and I was pushing. It was sure hard going in the sand and the weight of the wet hides made it even harder to move. We finally got the wagon out of the water; we pulled it up on the beach. We still had quite a ways to go before we were on some hard ground. Once we were on solid ground it went a little easier and we were able to get home with our wagon full of wet hide. When we got home mom helped us get it out of the wagon and hung it on a big branch of our tree in the shade to drip dry. What an ordeal. It took forever.

"What are we going to do with this?" I asked her.

She said "Well, we are going to make a pair of leggings. I'll show you how to sew beads on them after we cut them out and

I'll make you a pair after I get finished, so when you dance that is the only time you will wear them and I'll teach you how to take care of them." "I think I'm getting happy." I said "When are you going to show me how to do all this stuff?"

"Soon, come and I'll show you how to prepare the beads."

Once she had the beads all ready I said "Can I touch some of them?"

She said "No Dolly they aren't to play with and you might lose some then what would I do?"

Some time went by then one day she came and said "Come Dolly I have something to show you."

I went with her out doors and stood by the table and there before my eyes were all these beautiful beads. I put my hands behind my back like my Papadad did as to not touch them. It was really hard for me not to be able to pick one up. Before Chic started on her leggings she showed me and explained all the things that she had to do before she sewed the beads on the leather which was very soft and cuddly, I liked the feel of it. She laid one piece of hide down on the table and very precisely she placed certain beads in the areas in which she wanted them. When she finished with that she asked me to have a look and when I looked I saw designs of flowers and vines along the slit where she would tie it. She had placed four different colours of beads which were yellow, black, red and white.

I asked her "What do the different kinds of beads stand for?"

She said "They are the different people we are living with here on Mother Earth."

It took a long time for Chic to finish her leggings and when they were done they were beautiful. She also finished my dancing slippers which had a blue beaded flower on the foot and gathered around the top of the foot and even had fringe around the top. That's the first time I ever saw something like that and I remembered them all these years. She sat down on a stump and that was the first time in my life that I noticed her hands as I stood there beside her. On her right hand she had only a thumb and baby finger and on the left hand the third and fourth fingers were missing to the knuckle. This was not a handicap because she could bead, knit, sew, make bread, do anything anyone else could do. Mom never told me and no one ever talked about it until after Chic was gone. Mom said that she was born that way. In spite of having fingers missing she could do anything and she really did beautiful sewing. It didn't really matter what she was doing it was always done to the best of her ability and this is how she taught me to be. She would say 'Dolly you be and do things like that and don't ever give up, you see bringing your past forward and all the knowledge our people have is very important and should always remain as part of our lives, we can't go forward without remembering our past. Chic changed places in nineteen forty eight when I was seventeen years old at a time in my life when I needed her to be there because we had a lot of things yet to talk about. We were very close with each other from the time I was quite small and we never kept any secrets from each other. It was customary to mourn for a year after a loved one had gone. It wasn't the mourning part that bothered me, it was missing her. I found a huge void that I couldn't fill. Chic played a different role in my life than say my mother did, she was a very powerful woman. For instance her standing up for the rights of her people such as her telling me how hard she fought and argued not to have the government make us vote in the federal election; we never did. She was trying to teach us to live by our own system of government and this included the clan mothers picking the chiefs. She was quite vocal about a lot of issues. She was also very gentle and loving when it came time to deal with her family. I guess I'm like her in a way.

I've always been a strong supporter of our own way of life

and our own laws and trying to bring all these issues forward. Again it is who we are. I am very familiar with our great law and how it worked for us; it worked well two hundred years ago and it can work well for us now. There is more to being a Mohawk than in name only.

We are different than everyone else. These are some of the issues that I will continue to fight for. I for one do not want to be assimilated by the European culture. If you think about it we are the only people in Canada who have some person in Ottawa looking after our affairs. The immigrant people who live here always have had more rights and freedoms than the people who own this country. This is not acceptable to me.

Playing In The Hay Field

WHEN A CERTAIN TIME OF YEAR came around and there was a soft warm rain, it was the time of year when everything was sprouting up and growing fast. During this time Barb and I were allowed to go outside and jump up and down in the mud puddles with only our underwear on. There was this great big field that grew a lot of hay for the people who looked after the cows. After the hay was cut and taken into the barn, all the children who lived there ran down to the field. We seemed to be drawn to this field like magnets. It was a wonderful place to play and important that we had this area. It was really close to all our homes. As I look back now it was a field for all seasons, in the summer we played ball, tag and all sorts of other games. Even while the hay was growing and it was so high we played hide and seek in it. In the fall and winter we played on the frozen pond, built snow forts, skated. We had lots of fun. When it came around summer again and the puddles reappeared we took our canoes that papadad had made out of birch bark and held together with pine gum. This is where we spent a lot of our special time together when we were two little girls just having fun. I would take her by the hand and we took off running to see how many puddles we could find and which one would be the biggest, deepest and warmest. Barbara and I always had our birch bark canoes with us and we pretended all sorts of things. I'm sure we were out there for hours. Mom would come to the edge of the ditch where we saw her there and we waved at her, I'm sure she was just keeping an eye on us.

It was a long time after we were out there when Ila and Wilma Green came by to play with us. They didn't have a little canoe so we picked up some pieces of wood that was lying along the edge of the bush to use as canoes. We laid little stones in our canoes and they became our family. Sometimes the little canoe would tip over and all the people would fall out into the water; we picked some of the stones up and laid them on the ground to dry. This was our grandparents; we told them to wait there until we came back because we didn't have room for them this trip. We delivered the families to Point Anne because that was the only place we knew where to go. After the people got out of the canoe we would head back to the beach to pick up my parents. When we delivered them to Point Anne everyone was happy to see each other again. This trip to Point Anne was all imaginary because we were playing in puddles of water.

We were all having so much fun that we hadn't noticed an animal running along the edge of the bush where Peter Boots sometimes walked. We all stood up and looked at each other; we put our hands to our mouth and stood there very still and quite. We didn't know what it was.

Someone said "Maybe it was Peter Boot's dog."

I said "No, he doesn't have a dog."

We hung on hands and watched it for a long time. It walked along the edge of the bush then it would disappear. It came back out of the bush a ways from where it disappeared. We all thought it was playing hide and seek with us. It would stop and look at us for a minute then run a little ways up the path and disappear again. Just then we saw dad coming towards us; I guess he was wondering what we were doing.

We didn't move and we were still quiet as dad came closer and asked us "What's the matter?"

We still didn't say a word and then I spoke and said "There some kind of animal running along the bush where Peter Boots walks all the time. We didn't know what it was."

Just then out it came from the bush again and this time dad saw it. Dad knelt down and we all did the same, he explained what it was in a whisper,

"It's a coyote but we call it God's dog."

I asked "Why did you tell us in a whisper?"

"Because I didn't want to scare him away" dad said "don't ever be afraid of him, he won't hurt you. It's like a dog but you always remember it's a wild animal and to always respect it. He has the freedom to run where ever he wants so I would like you to always care for this animal and don't ever harm him. Creator put him here to live with us and all other animals as well."

My dad was a wonderful father, he always had time for people whether little or big and a loving person and very soft spoken. He was even a father to his brother's children. He was a spiritual person and he taught us how to care and love each other and showed us the importance of the ceremonies I was always taught to remember. I am passing on some of my knowledge about what I have learned and who taught me and I'll be forever grateful. I love you, dad.

Papadad Sorting Potatoes

Sitting on a stump in the door yard was my papadad who was blind and I was too young to know what blindness meant. He wore dark glasses night and day whether sunny or cloudy. He was waiting for mom to bring another basket of potatoes to be sorted for planting and had been there for a long time wanting to know why the basket was still empty. Once in a while he'd pick up the basket and run his arm around inside it to try to find out what was going on. Finally he called mom over and asked her,

"Why are there no potatoes in the basket?"

Mom said laughing "Papadad, if you could see what the girls have been doing."

"What have they done?" he asked.

Barbara and I thought he was playing with us and every time he cut a potato and threw it in the basket, we'd pick it out and throw it on the ground. We were sitting right there at his feet not making any sound.

He asked mom "Am I missing the basket?"

He didn't know what Barbara and I had been doing up to this point.

"They have taken every potato that you have cut and threw

them all over the door yard."

Papadad laughed and said "Wait 'til I get a hold of you two, I'll tickle you until you say ants are my uncles."

Barb and I just started laughing.

Papadad was the potato sorter in our family; he wanted to feel needed and besides he was the head of the family. I remember him sitting there on a stump for long periods of time, I thought he was resting. Once in a while he would get up and walk around to stretch his legs waving his cane as he walked. My job was to lead him by the hand back to his favorite stump. He started sorting potatoes again and Barbara and I had a big job to do picking up every potato that we had thrown on the ground and put them back in the basket. I took his hand and placed it on the basket, he laughed and said,

"Oh my, it got full fast. Can I get you and Barb to help me with all the rest of my chores? What do you think of that idea?"

We said "Oh sure."

Papadad sat there for a little while longer sorting potatoes while Barbara and I had to make sure we had found all the potatoes we had thrown away before we finished for the day. Later after we had eaten our night time meal I remember sitting on Papadads knee and I told him,

"I am sorry for throwing the potatoes all over the door yard, we were just playing."

"I know that." he said, "I was little once and I probably did the same things you are doing."

Before going to bed I hugged and kissed him and told him,

"I would help him tomorrow."

"Okay Dolly, night night."

The next day papadad and I were up early and tried to get each other something to eat but I was too little and he was blind. We did manage to make enough noise to wake everyone else up. After we had eaten papadad asked me,

"Are you ready to go to work again?"

I said "Oh yes.

We were out there for a while before we had one basket filled and I asked,

"What do you want me to do with the full basket?"

"Don't throw them around the door yard again." he said, "can you just drag them over by the summer kitchen?"

"Okay"

I worked hard at dragging this basket, it was heavy. I must have been gone for a while because papadad wanted to know where I was.

I grunted saying "I'm over here."

Papadad told me "We would have to wait until the potatoes got a little soft and wrinkly before we plant them"

I said "Like grandma?"

He hollered and laughed so hard and he scared me half to death, mom came running out of the house to see what had happened. Papadad was just jumping up and down; he couldn't seem to stop laughing. He must have wiped his eyes out a hundred times with his red and white polka dot handkerchief. I have never seen my grandfather laugh so hard, he didn't even lose his cap. Mom took him by the hand and asked,

"What's wrong?" He began to explain to mom what happened word for word. Mom just looked at me with her head cocked to one side, her hand to her mouth and tears in her eyes and hugged papadad and said

"We will never repeat this, okay?"

Papadad couldn't answer for laughing, he just nodded. I really didn't know why they were so happy. Mom said to me,

"Don't tell anyone, this is our secret." That was the first time I ever shared a secret or knew what the word meant.

"Are you going to help me plant the potatoes when the time comes?" Papadad asked.

"Oh yes." I said.

We always have a lot of fun when we are out in the field planting anything. He taught me a lot about planting. Mother Earth has to be prepared; things that you plant have to be watered. Our garden had to be kept clean. I didn't realize that all these things I was helping with were lessons until I was a little older. The time had come to plant our potatoes. Dad hitched our horse to the wooden plough. I took the potatoes in our little wagon and papadad went with the horse who knew exactly where it was going because he had done this task many many times. Papadad and the horse started the furrow and he always said to me,

"Eyes up!"

"Okay." I said.

We planted all the potatoes that he had sorted.

I've learned a lot about how to survive; I always remembered it was easy because I had lived it. I'm so fortunate to have been born into this family and my Mohawk culture has made me very strong. I am continuing to live my life as a Mohawk woman, not living in limbo any more; it is who I am. I have brought a lot of things forward with me; I'm a very determined person. I'll never let my language, spirituality or culture vanish. Even planting our garden and doing everyday living it was a wonderful time for me to be growing up in a place I loved so much and the people are still a big part of my life.

Aunt Elisha

—————➤●◄—————

THE EVENTS THAT OCCURRED IN THIS story happened when I was young and living on the territory. Elisha was my grandmother Chic's sister and she would visit us from time to time unannounced. On one of these visits she decided to stay for a few days which pleased Chic because they got along very well together. After the night time meal was cleaned up and some chatting went on everyone decided to go to bed. She slept downstairs on a tick in the parlor on the floor beside the stove. We three girls and our parents and Chic were all sleeping upstairs. It was a beautiful clear night; the moon was shining through the window in our bedroom. Some time in the middle of the night our cat, who never ever came in the house some how sneaked in and went right upstairs looking for a warm place to sleep by the stove pipe. This was when the cat decided to relieve itself and when it did my aunt was in the line of fire.

"Budge! Budge! The roof is leaking! Make sure you fix it tomorrow." Elisha yelled.

Dad told her, "Be quiet, you'll have all the Indians on the reserve up."

But she wouldn't be quiet. Dad took our lamp and went

downstairs to see what was bothering her. She repeated,

"It's raining!"

Dad said "No! it's a clear night and the moon is shining."

Now everyone was downstairs to see what was going on and dad was trying to find out what was leaking. It took quite a while but mom figured what had happened, our cat ran downstairs nearly knocking Chic down, dad opened the door and out he went. After Elisha found out what had happened she was some upset and decided she was going home now! It wasn't daylight when she left, Chic tried talking her into staying but she had her mind made up, she was leaving.

Sometime later, perhaps a year, aunt Elisha came back for another visit. I saw her coming up the lane and I ran up to the house and told mom. She told us not to tease her and make her cross. Dad was working for a farmer I think he was helping to cut hay and when he came home from working he saw aunt Elisha. He was going to say something but my mom was very quick to put her finger to her mouth to remind dad to keep quiet, we all knew it was killing him to say something. She asked dad,

"What do you want me to do to help seeing that you worked all day and you are tired?"

"Well we have three cows that haven't been milked yet." Dad said.

So she decided to milk the cows.

Dad said, "You don't have to do that."

She said "I can do that." She wouldn't take no for an answer. She picked up the two milk pails and headed for the barn. As she went out the door, dad was standing in the doorway trying to tell her that we had a jersey cow that didn't like to be milked.

"Remember," dad said, "you have to tie her two hind legs together. There's a strap hanging on a nail just beside her." Dad was quite concerned the cow might kick and hurt her, but as she was walking down towards the barn she hollered,

"Don't worry; I've milked many a cow long before you were born."

Dad said, "Yea, yea, but not like this one."

Dad went to get washed up for our night time meal and he mentioned to mom,

"Maybe I should go to the barn to see how she's making out."

Mom said, "Don't do that, she'll be back any minute now!"

Just then mom heard some racket outside and looked out the window and told dad,

"Here she comes."

"She didn't bring the milk pails back." Dad said, "and she looks like she's upset with the world."

When she came in the house mom asked her, "What's happened?"

She just looked at my mom and never said a word. When she turned around she had fresh cow chips all over her clothes,

"Don't ask me what happened, I'll tell you! I sat down on the stool, patted the cow on the hip and told her 'I'm not Budge'; she just turned her head and looked at me with those big brown eyes. I put the milk pail between my knees, gently pulled on her udder. The first sound was the milk hitting the pail then me hitting the floor right where she'd made a mess. I looked at her and said 'I don't cars if your udders blow up or not I'm gone'."

Dad asked her, "Did you tie the belt around her hind legs?"

"No, I forgot!"

After she calmed down somewhat, she decide to stay for supper and for the night. The next day was a replica of the day before. Chic came over to visit and everyone was talking about what had happened. Elisha told everyone,

"The next time I come over here it will only be to visit; I won't be doing any favors."

Mom said "That's a good idea."

Chic piped up and said "The place is jinxed; every time you come here something happens. You're getting too old to be kicked around by a cow. So just come to visit next time and none of this will happen."

Elisha lived to be one hundred and one.

A Winter At The Beach

ONE WINTER WHILE LIVING AT THE beach I recall walking down to the bay with my dad so that I could bring back his snow shoes after he put on his skates. There was a large willow tree at the beach which had a limb that grew low over the ground so that even I could sit on it in the winter and dad used this limb to sit on to change into his skates. Dad gave me his snow shoes, picked me up and kissed me on my brow head and he said,

"You can go back home now".

As I turned and started to walk away I turned back around again facing the bay to watch my dad skating hard and going really fast. I shouted at him and hollered,"I love you daddy", but he was too far out on the bay to hear me. I cried all the way home.

When I got home I asked mom "Where is daddy going?"

She picked me up and sat me on the table facing her and held my face in her hands and told me,

"Don't cry any more, dad's going to work in Point Anne and he will be back home at our night time meal."

"Then can I go and meet him?"

"Yes, because you'll have to take his snow shoes back down to the bay so he can walk home with you again."

I seem to be quite satisfied when I knew everything was all right. Papadad tried to keep me busy. We were playing a game called 'Jail' we created. He would grab me when I ran by and hold me between his knees and I remember tearing paper off the wall to pay my way out of jail. We were having a lot of fun until mom came by.

She asked me "What are you doing?"

"I'm in jail and I have to pay papadad to get out".

He thought this was kind of funny but mom didn't.

"Maybe we shouldn't be playing this game any more." he said.

I remember flopping both my arms forward and saying "Now what are we going to do?" Papada said "After our night time meal I'll make some more animals from the light of the lamp and you can tell me what they are."

Just then mom came and kissed me on the head and said,

"It's time to get ready to go and meet dad and don't forget to take his snow shoes."

She tied my snow shoes on my feet and off I went down to the bay to meet dad. I was there for a little while and I thought he forgot to come home or he got lost. Soon I looked up and saw someone out on the bay and I hid behind the big willow tree and didn't come out until I knew it was my dad. The first thing I said was,

"I love you and I thought you got lost."

He asked me "What did you do all day'?

I told him "Papadad and I were playing jail and mom caught me pulling paper off the wall and she wasn't too happy."

Dad said "Everything is ok now".

Dad got washed up and we had our night time meal. Mom had deer stew that aunt Ina had given us and we had some elder berries that Chic and I picked earlier in the year. It sure felt good that I contributed. Mom poured them over our hot fry bread, mmm, was it good.

I asked "Can I talk to Creator?"

Papadad said "Yes, Dolly. This is the first time she has asked for this important permission"

I thanked Creator for showing my dad the right way home and special thanks for the deer we were having and also for the elder berries that chic and I had picked. I looked out the window to see if the maple tree was moving and I told papadad ,

"Creator didn't hear me".

Papadad said "Oh yes he did."

I hugged my dad and he had tears in his eyes, he told me "Creator always listens to everyone."

That was quite an evening. We did watch papadad make all sorts of animals on the wall from the light of the lamp and we had to tell him what they were.

I said "That's a cow."

He just laughed and said "No, no, no, I can't make cows."

We went to bed happy that night with a full belly.

The next morning dad and I did the same thing all over again. This was around the same time that Barbara and I had learned to walk pretty good in our new snow shoes but she never went with me to meet dad at the beach when he came home from working all day in Point Anne. Both my parents worked hard to make sure everyone was comfortable and had enough to eat. I know my dad was tired when he got home because he lay on the floor by the stove and went to sleep before he had his night time meal. Mom and grandma always liked us to eat together and we did because it was important to be together as a family.

During the day Barb and I were asked to bring some wood in for the night. We piled it in the summer kitchen and mom said we were helping dad. Even papadad helped us, he stayed in the summer kitchen and told barb and I where to pile the wood by feeling around in certain areas. Dad appreciated what we did because he thanked us for doing a really good job. Papadad made sure we had enough water to last all night. I tried to chop a hole in the well but couldn't so papadad said he would help me but I would have to take him out to the well because he was blind. Before we left the summer kitchen where dad had stored all his tools to go to the well I was supposed to bring a big iron rod that papadad could use to punch a hole in the ice. When we got to the well I gave him the rod which worked out okay. That's the first time I can remember that papadad had his ear flappers down over his ears so it must have been cold. We had a lot of snow that time but it was good. We did get the water okay. Papadad asked me to put him on the path that led to the toilet; so I took him by the hand and when we got to the toilet I put his hand on the toilet door. While I waited for him he gave me his cap to wear 'til he was ready to go back home. I was so pleased, I just loved his cap.

He asked me "How far are we from the house to the toilet?"

I said "A mile and a quarter."

"It didn't take us long to get here."

I said "No because you said hurry up."

"Are we on the same path going home?"

I said "We are but we have to walk backwards."

Papadad asked "Why?"

"We are just playing."

"Shall we hurry up, because I'm cold, aren't you?"

"Huh, huh."

When we got back in the house grandma asked us what took so long and papadad said because Dolly said it was a mile and a quarter to the toilet and grandma laughed and hugged the both of us. She said you two are pretty good buddies and he said Dolly's a Lewis through and through and she's my right hand man.

These times are all so special. This is why I'm so determined to bring all this forward, the stories, ceremonies and what it was really like at my home at Tyendinaga and I know now that my dad must have been tired having to skate to Point Anne and work all day then skate back home and look after his family.

A Trip To Shannonville

WE ALWAYS WALKED TO SHANNONVILLE AND some times I'm sure it was to meet mom. It was always in the dark and dad was always with us. Between Beverly Brant's and Fred Lewis place there was a special spot that had long rows of bushes growing there and there were mullens on the side of the gravel road that wasn't too wide. To a little girl they looked like a small forest of little trees some of which were even taller than I was. This is the spot where dad would ask us if we had to go in the bush, and of course we did. He always picked us a fuzzy leaf from a plant called a mullen and gave one to each of us to use when we finished. As we came out of the bush there were two people walking behind us going towards the village then turned and started to go towards the bush, so I picked two mullen leaves and started to run towards them.

Dad hollered "Where are you going?"

I told him "Two people were going into the bush and I wanted to give them a leaf."

Dad said "No! No! They have to get their own leaves."

This is where dad hid our wagon and lantern and it was because we had to sneak into the village and I recall doing this a lot. After we came out of the bush we stopped at Marshal Lewis' so dad could visit and we could wash our hands. There were some people in the village who screamed at us to get back in the bush and dad never did say anything but we always were quiet and sneaked around certain areas that we walked in and we always went the same way. I recall running over the Salmon River bridge one evening and dad told us to hide on the other side. We thought dad was playing hide and seek with us but he came under the bridge with us and told us to be quiet. A car was coming slowly towards the bridge and dad thought it was the Indian agent out on patrol. The agent did this a lot and we had no letter from him and dad knew what that meant. It wasn't just us who went somewhere without a letter. Everyone else was doing the same thing, and all the people had trouble with the Indian agent since he wasn't there for our benefit. I recall mom sold some strawberries to people who came and stayed at the bay and someone had told the Indian agent and he came and told mom that she owed him some money for the berries. That's the only time I remember dad telling him to leave our property. I remembered all these atrocities when I got older and became very bitter and to this day I still feel hurt and I'm supposed to forgive these people of whom there were many; I don't think so. Mom was working at the canning factory and when we saw her, dad would leave us three girls with mom because he had to work all night. Then mom and us three girls would walk back home to the beach, mom carrying the lantern, Barb and I pulling the wagon with Carmel in it. I remember being very tired when we arrived home. This is when we three were allowed to sleep with mom in her bed when dad worked all night.

Today when my husband and I are out walking or driving and see the mullen plant he always laughs when I mention it to him since he knows all about this event. I have to pick one leaf and just feel how soft it is and it brings back all the memories of living at Mohawk Beach and how important this place is to me; good memories I'll cherish for ever.

A Visit From Aunt Emma

————➤●◄————

I'LL INTRODUCE YOU TO MY AUNT Emma. She was my dad's older sister, a milliner by trade, married to Herkimer Brant and had one son whose name was Kenneth. He was married to Marjorie Claus. They had several children and lived just West of Church Lane on Highway Two on the North side. I remember visiting them quite often. Their children and we were the same age. One of their children, a girl, was killed by a hit and run driver. My cousin Peter was with her at the time walking home from school. I guess she died instantly. Peter had a hard time getting over it. I remember going to her wake with my parents. I didn't realize exactly what was going on; there were a lot of people at the house. I recalled her parents crying a lot and my parents trying to comfort them. I don't know whether they ever knew who did this horrible thing or if it was ever investigated. This was aunt Emma's grandchild, we called her aunt Bobbi.

Quite some time later aunt Bobbi went back to Toronto where she worked and we never heard from her for a while. Everyone was worried for her and of course my family had no way to get in touch with her to see if she was all right. The family discussed her being away and decided she would know when to come home again and soon after she showed up. We were all glad to see her. When she came in she had a suitcase and after a few days passed she showed us what was in the case. She had brought me a pair of shoes. I always had to work hard for what ever I got.

She said "If you can put these shoes on by yourself you can keep them."

I don't know how long it took me but it was a long time and I finally prevailed. I wouldn't take them off, I'm sure I wore them to bed. I remember getting up the next morning still wearing my shoes. These little shoes were made of black shiny leather with a wee round button on the outside of the shoe with a small strap you had to put through a slit in the tongue. I also recall trying so hard to dance with them on but my feet kept sticking to the floor. She noticed the hard time I was having trying to dance, and told me "Next time I come home I will bring you a pair of dancing shoes."

It seemed she was gone for a long time again and me patiently waiting for my shoes. Finally she returned to see us all and this time she brought a whole lot of stuff with her. She had something for everyone. She laid everything out on the table except my shoes. Dad got some rosin for his fiddle bow. Papadad only had a stick when we went for a walk so he got a real cane. Grandma Rose got a new apron, and mom got a new hat.

Mom said "Are you trying to make me look like a queen?"

She finally gave me my new dancing shoes. They had something on the toe and heal. "What are these things?" I asked her.

She told me "They make a nice beat when you are dancing."

She had a dress for each of my sisters. That was the first time that I had new shoes that came from a store.

"Now I have two pair of shoes, one for walking with papadad and a special pair for dancing."

I put on my new shoes and dad played the fiddle and I danced for her before she went back to work. The reason I remembered what everyone got is because she told me,

"Have a look and try to remember what things you saw on the table, if you can remember I would win a big prize."

I remembered and the big prize was my dancing shoes that were on the table.

She made an announcement that I had won the prize and it was my new shoes. The first pair she brought me I wore when I took papadad for a walk and was very careful where I walked because I didn't want to get my shoes dirty. When I went to bed I put my dancing shoes right beside me where I was sleeping then I'd take them back down stairs next morning in case I was going to dance.

Aunt Bobbi stayed a while visiting with my parents and grand parents. She looked a lot like my dad. There was a fiddling contest going on one time when she was home and I don't ever remember seeing so many fiddlers at once; I didn't know who to watch first. This event I remember quite clearly, my uncle had killed a deer and he had given us some. Mom had a big pot of deer stew, a big pan of fry bread and a big iron pot full of corn soup and some canned peaches that mom had preserved. Dad attended the fire in the door yard and a lot of people were there including her son Kenny, Marjorie and their children. I remember standing beside her holding her around the waist and she had tears of joy in her eyes. Looking back now I really wish I had a camera but I guess we weren't supposed to take pictures. I really enjoyed aunt Bobbi, she was a huggy person like I am and she was funny, always teasing my dad and he would tease her too. These times may be past but they will always be in my mind and in my heart. We as Mohawk people have had an awful lot of things taken from us but this is something that no one will ever be able to take, our memories. What power we have to be able to maintain our culture and all the things that make us who we are through our Mohawk stories. Aunt Bobbi was talking to daddy and papadad later and said,

"I am quite surprised that Margaret can remember so well. She should be taught about our ways because she has such a good memory and always remembers what she has been taught. According to our laws the teachings have to be handed down to a woman and maybe she will be our link in the future to keep Tyendinaga alive."

A Bad Storm

I THINK IT MIGHT HAVE BEEN spring; it was one of those kinds of days that were warm and still and even our dog, beauty, was acting strange. She would run in and out of the house several times and whine a lot and go outside and lay under the tree like she was sick. Dad said to mom "Something not very pleasant is going to happen today." Dad kept us all busy doing what ever we had to do to prepare ourselves for whatever was going to happen. I remember dad had helped uncle Oliver Hill put some hay in the barn that day. This barn didn't have a door because it was taken to the beach by a team of horses and a lumber wagon to dance on. It got quite hot and mom sent me with a honey pail of water to where dad was in the hay field. I remember he drank some and poured some on his head. Sometime later dad was on his way home and I went to meet him. When we got home he spent some time talking to papadad in the door yard. It must have been serious talk because I didn't go over and dad was bent over listening to his father. I was in the house trying to help mom with our night time meal and I said

"It gets dark out then it gets daylight again and can I go down to the bay?"

She said "Don't be long and take the dog."

This time the dog didn't want to go like she usually would and I had to coax her. Her body language was saying lets go home. We finally got to the water's edge and I had never seen the water look like that. There was a very strong wind and there were big waves on the bay; I didn't know what was going on and I was scared for Chic because I knew she lived over that way. I turned and ran towards the house and the dog passed me like an arrow, she was glad to go home. The wind had died down somewhat and dad was outdoors fixing our sacred fire.

"What are you doing?" I asked, "Are we having a ceremony?"

Dad said "Yes."

Dad and I walked around the corner of the house and took a look down towards the bay. We heard one crack of thunder. Dad told me to go in the house, and then he went and got papadad who was sitting on a stump and took him in the house.

Papadad told dad "Take the little ones and go in the house now."

Dad said "Everyone is in."

Dad told mom he didn't like the look of the sky, it was a funny colour and Papadad overheard my dad tell mom. We were all supposed to lie down on the floor. The dog started whining and dad told us to go pet the dog.

The wind started blowing really hard and the sky was really black, it was like night time. The rains came down with hail, I never saw this before and I thought it was balls falling outside. I wanted to go out and get some but mom said we can't do that right now. Mom and dad were watching out the summer kitchen window. We weren't allowed near the window.

Dad said "There goes our maple tree."

There were other things flying around outside. We girls were crying hanging onto mom and dad.

We asked them "Are we going to be okay?"

Mom said "Yes."

Just then the wind blew so hard that it blew the big window right out of the house. Mom got a quilt off the bed and she and dad were trying to hold it in the widow so our roof wouldn't go. In the meantime they're telling Barbara and me to get under the bed and take Carmel with us. Barb got under first pulling Carmel and me pushing and we were hugging each other and crying.

After it was all over I remember dad saying it was a good thing it didn't last too long and I never saw a storm like that. I didn't know if it was time to go to bed or stay up. I ran to papadad's bedroom and he and grandma had a blanket in their window. I asked them if they were okay and they said they were fine.

Papadad said "Go and get your little sisters and come and visit grandma and I for a while." I remember shaking.

Papadad said "Everything is okay; we will talk to Creator now."

I remember not wanting to go to bed. Mom would put us girls to bed all together; we woke up crying a lot of the time. Because of the storm we had bad dreams for quite a while. That was one time I recall grandma Rose using her turtle rattle and we had a lot of healing ceremonies.

There was a lot of damage done at the beach. Uncle Oliver lost most of his barn and a cow got killed, a big tree had fallen on it. Our house was damaged too. After it was over the elders decided to have a ceremony. We all gathered with the rest of the people to give thanks for our safety. It was quite emotional. I don't know if they ever remembered being in one of these storms and I can honestly say to this day I can remember. Dad heard later it had been a tornado. That was the first time that I can remember our Sacred fire was not burning; it was blown out by the wind and all our sacred things were strewn all over the door yard. Before we could have the ceremony dad had to clean the area of debris because it was always to be kept clean. It took dad a long time to do this job and mom helped him. We girls were not allowed to help so papadad kept us busy. As far as I can remember we finally did have a ceremony, two to be exact. The first one was for the thunder, I don't know how long that took and the second one was to thank the Creator for watching over us all who lived at the beach and for everyone else who might have gone through it. Dad wanted us to remember how powerful these storms are and what can happen here on Mother Earth and that these are all natural events. The people all came to help. Dad and I went to different houses to make sure everyone else was okay and as far as we knew no human lost their life and for that we were all thankful and that we were all together again. I'll never forget that storm. It took dad quite a while to fix our house again. Everybody was good and did what ever they could to help each other out. Things go better when we all work together. This is the way we should be living today, by trying to help each other and by just being there. Remember the things we've learned and do them every day. This is what our people did a long time ago in order to survive.

Our Big Black Iron Pot

THIS POT WAS HUGE, IT TOOK my mom and grandmother to pick it up and put it on the stove. They would only use this pot when something was happening. After they got it on the stove they removed one lid and sat the pot in the hole. The first thing to go into the pot was pork hocks and a lot of water. I got up on a chair and looked in the pot, I had never seen so many pigs' feet.

I asked grandma, "Where's the rest of the pig?"

She kissed me on the forehead and told me to go see if I could find them. So I went searching for a bunch of pigs with no feet. The first place I went was to Uncle Oliver Hill's farm. I went straight for the pig pen. I sat on an old wooden fence. He came out of the house carrying two pails and asked me,

"What are you doing?"

I said" Looking at the pigs."

"Do they look funny?" he asked me.

I said "No, but they all have their feet."

"Why are you looking at their feet?"

"Because grandma and mom have a big pot full of pigs feet and I was wondering where they got them."

He said "You better get down; you might fall in and hurt

my pigs."

He just laughed at me and gave me a basket of eggs to take home to mom. So on my way home I visited other people who had pigs to see if they all had their feet. These people just looked at me and smiled.

Finally when I got home grandma asked me "Where have you been, you've been gone for a long time?"

I told her where I went and what I was doing.

She said "Did you find any pigs?"

I said "Yes, but they all had their feet."

It turned out that dad had been given some pig feet from pigs someone else had slaughtered.

I asked mom "Where's dad?"

"He and papadad are smoking some pork to make bacon, they'll be home shortly."

When dad and papadad came home I asked dad "How many feet does a pig have?"

He said "Four, why?"

"Because grandma and mom are cooking the big iron pot full of pig's feet and I can't find the rest of the pigs."

He jumped and picked me up and said "You're silly Dolly."

Then he just laughed.

I was trying to figure out how many pigs were missing from the number of feet in the pot. I tried counting them but I couldn't.

Mom finally told me "There were four pigs."

"Oh mom, there are all those pigs out there with no feet."

Mom said "No honey, your uncle Jimmy and aunt Winnie helped some people put some pigs to sleep and they were kind enough to give us one."

I said "Okay, are we going to have some fry bread and corn soup too?"

"We are going to have a feast."

"What's a feast?"

"That's when we have a lot of food and a lot of people to share it with."

"Are we having this now?" I asked mom.

"Yes" mom said "Would you take papadad and get some cabbage, potatoes and some carrots?"

"Okay."

I went to get papadad who was sitting on a stump in the door yard whittling. It didn't take long for me to get distracted, I was supposed to take papadad to get some vegetables but I was more interested in what papadad was doing for quite a while and of course I had to return to the house to ask mom what I was supposed to be getting for her. After she told me again I went and got papadad and took him by the hand and told him what we were supposed to get from the garden. This mission we were on took a little more time because we were just strolling along the path that led to the garden.

Papadad said "We better hurry Dolly and get the things mom sent us after".

I let go of papadads hand suddenly.

He asked me "What are you doing?"

I told him "I see something."

"What is it?" he asked.

"I don't know "I said.

He was asking all sorts of questions that I didn't know the answers to.

I asked papadad "Don't move and stand right here and I will be right back".

I ran back to the house to get mom. I was looking down the path in front of me and there were all these little things just kind of slithering along the path. I squatted down to have a good look. It looked at me with little round dark eyes and was sticking out its tongue really fast.

Finally I got mom and she asked me "What's wrong?"

"I don't know."

As I was running backwards ahead of her on the path I told her "These little things were sticking out their tongues and saying lather, lather, lather really fast. They are a lather animal."

When she saw them she told me "They are little lizards." She told me "Don't hurt them." I said "No, no."

So I ran carefully on the path and told papadad "They were lather lizards."

Papadad smiled and said "Okay."

We journeyed on the path holding hands and brought back the vegetables that mom needed. I went back out and watched the lather lizards for a while until they finally crawled off in the long grass and I never played very much in that area because I didn't want to step on them. When I came back outdoors I told papadad that it smells real good in the house.

He said "I could smell it when you opened the door."

As time went on papadad finished what he was creating.

"Before I give you your flute I'll show you where to put your little fingers to make it sound like music."

It was a small flute and the holes were closer together than a normal flute. I remember trying so hard to make some kind of sound come from it but I did have fun. I marched from the house all the way down to the bay.

I even stopped at grandpa Cons to show him what papadad had made for me. He suggested I learn to play Turkey in the Straw.

"Okay." I said as I started hopping, skipping and jumping down the narrow path that led to the water. I had a lot of fun playing my flute; I even learned how to play Three Blind Mice, at least my dad recognized most of the sounds. Music was always a big part of our family. Both my dad and papadad played the fiddle, grandma Rose could play the piano. This is some of the things that happened at my house when I lived at the beach. It didn't seem to matter what happened, we always tried to stay positive. I think it was expected of the elders to make sure the children always had good thoughts. I had for the most part a wonderful childhood. I was free from worries and didn't really know that any other place ever existed.

While mom and grandma were getting the vegetables ready, papadad said "Come Dolly, I'll tell you a story about a little girl looking for lost pigs."

I laughed and said "That's a story about me."

He laughed hard too, and he hugged me. By this time it was night and someone had lit the only lamp we had and set it on the table. Finally a lot of people arrived. Everyone was having a grand old time while we were eating. Papadad made some pictures on the wall by the shadow of the lamp.

He said "Do you know what it is?"

I remember telling him it was a whole bunch of pigs with no feet. He just dropped his hands and started tapping his feet on the floor laughing,

I don't remember what the event was about but a lot of people came and brought something to eat and we really did have a feast. I remember Uncle Oliver and his family coming and they had brought some other part of the pig. Boy, what a wonderful time we had. It turned out to be just a visiting time. They really liked my grandma and papadad, we were all very close and we took care of each other and we had a lot of respect for everyone. I miss these times and what we did and living where I lived.

My Mom and Dad

Let me introduce you to my mother whose name was Kathleen Sero and she came from a long line of Mohawk people as did my dad whose name was Gordon Lewis. They were married at Tyendinaga in March of nineteen twenty two. Dad met mom at the church with his horse and buggy on their wedding day. Before they took their vows a train went by and blew its whistle, scared the horse which took off down the road with the buggy in tow. Dad left mom at the alter and chased the horse until he caught it. When he finally came back everyone else was waiting for him so the rites for my parents resumed. After they were wed everyone sat down in the church and had a real good laugh. The minister's name was Mr. Keegan who told the wedding party "I have married a lot of people in my time but this is the first time a wedding has held so much excitement." They had been married for a long time before I came along and were living at Point Anne for a while since dad was employed at the Canada Cement Plant, later on he and mom took up residence at Mohawk Beach to look after his parents.

I remember when I was little living on a reserve in Ontario named Tyendinaga. Our mom and dad worked in a canning factory in Shannonville. They started in the summer when the fruit was ripe up until the time to can tomatoes. The factory was located on the North side of the Salmon River and at peak canning time the wagons that would be loaded five crates high blocked the road going from the York Road and the Beach Road heading into the canning factory. The amount of tomatoes coming in required that the factory ran twenty-four hours a day. The tomato cans were labelled 'Miss Canada' and I remember the colour yet. I'm sure that all the people who were eligible to work from the Mohawk community were hired. Dad worked nights and mom worked days and dad would sleep in the daytime then about ten o'clock at night he would say,

"Let's go meet mom"

We would take our lantern with the wagon which we used to pull Carmel home. Mom would visit with some of her friends before we headed home and we kissed and hugged our dad. Dad would light the lantern for mom and we would start walking down the Beach Road singing not realizing that our mom was tired. When we got home we would all go to bed right away.

All the people had to get their flour at the gristmill and also they received five dollars for each person and this had to last us all year. We took our bag of flour home on a wagon that dad had hidden in the bushes near uncle Marshall's corn field on the Beach Road. A few days after getting the flour mom was going to make some bread and found that the flour was full of little black bugs and we couldn't use it. When we took it back to Shannonville the person who was working at the gristmill said that he couldn't help us so dad and mom and we three girls went to Deseronto to see the Indian agent. His big concern was how we got there without a note. This letter was issued to everyone who wanted to go anywhere, we even had to produce this letter to visit our family who lived in different areas on the same reserve; I'm so glad that we were so important that they had to keep track of us in this way. I knew nothing of this letter until one day papadad got sick and dad had to get a letter to take him to the doctor. I could imagine all sorts of things happening such as before you got back with the letter someone could have died and maybe this happened, what an awful way to treat people.

With all the injustices that were brought upon us in the hopes of assimilation, it must really tick the government off to see that we are surviving. What a battle we are fighting. I will never be taken in by these people or anyone else.

Dad didn't answer the agent, mom had taken some flour with her to show him, and he looked at it and said,

"What can I do about it?"

Mom was feisty by this time and asked him,

"Would you eat it?"

She got no answer. Then we left and went back home. On the way back home we met other people and found out that everyone on the reserve had the same problem with the flour. Mom said that other people were going to complain to the Indian agent but I don't remember if anything ever happened. Since we didn't have any wheat flour for the year, mom and my two grandmothers ground up the white-floured corn we had to use whenever they needed flour. They worked at grinding the corn; it was all done by hand. Mom used the flour that was ground up every day. To grind the corn they put it in a thick cloth and hammered it until it was almost as fine as flour; this was done as often as needed. I'm sure everyone was doing the same thing. There seemed to be no end to what we had to do just to survive day by day. I have never seen any other people so determined to survive in the European world and make it as the aboriginal people have. We have fought all our lives for a few pittances that the white government has given us each year; think about all the resources taken from native land with no benefit going to my people. Is it so hard for the white people to own up to the truth of what really happened? My sisters and I knew nothing of the hardships that were forced upon our people until we were older.

We had a tough life but there was always lots of love and caring and we got through it okay keeping our sanity.

Our Rain Barrel

Outside our kitchen door we had two big iron rain barrels that had a purple tinge to them and a big barb on one side of the rim. Mom used the rain water to wash our hair and it never seemed to be empty. Dad made a wooden cover for each barrel with a leather handle to make it easier to pick the lid up. The covers were there to keep the dirt out of the water but I really think it was there to keep us from playing in the water. One day when Barbara and I were out playing and chasing each other I came upon an old beaver pelt that we had been playing with earlier in the year, I must have chased her around the house three or four times whacking her with the pelt. We got tired and just laid down in the long grass and laughed. After we rested for a while I urged her to run again so I could chase her; she ran around the corner of the house out of sight and as I came to the same corner I had the beaver pelt in my left hand and I smacked the rain barrel with it and it got stuck on the barb and I never let go. I kept right on running and the jolt caused both feet to leave the ground and I skinned both my knees in the gravel that dad had shoveled there to set the barrel on and I was wondering what hit me. Mom came out of the house to see what had happened and of course the pelt was floating in the rain barrel. She took a look and didn't know what it was. In the meantime Barbara was hiding on me on the other side of the house and mom didn't see or know where she was and she thought I was still chasing her; Barbara really didn't know what had happened. I tried to explain what was in the rain barrel but mom wouldn't listen, she was upset. She finally calmed down enough so I could tell her what was going on and she just sat on the stump bent over with her head in her hands. I remember mom shaking a little bit when she was crying. I asked her,

"What was wrong?"

She held me and kissed me on the cheek and said, "You sure scared me."

I said, "I'm sorry."

She thought my sister had fallen in the rain barrel. Just then Chic came out the door inquiring what was going on and mom said I'll tell you later.

Those two rain barrels reminded me of a lot of things that went on at our house like the time papadad told us about the cow that got chased by the moon clear across the sky. I laughed and asked papadad,

"What happened to the cow, was it ours?"

Papadad said, "No, it wasn't our cow. When the moon saw it's reflection in the rain barrel it noticed the cow was running so fast and its tongue was hanging out and its legs were flying in all different directions that the moon felt sorry for the cow and stopped suddenly and the cow smacked into the moon. Now if you look closely at the moon you can see the cow and that's where we get our green cheese from."

"I'll never eat cheese again." I said.

Mom picked the pelt out of the barrel which by now was really soaked and when she flung it some of the water flew off in big drops and hit papadad square in the face.

He asked mom, "Is it raining?"

Mom couldn't answer him because she was laughing so hard. Mom told him, "No, it's not raining but you stood right in the line of fire."

When she let go of the pelt it landed it our maple tree in the front door yard. I was laughing so hard I had my hands between my knees.

"What are you laughing at?" Mom asked.

"We have a wet beaver in the tree."

Everyone just roared with laughter. During all the commotion papadad said,

"Go get my fiddle; we're going to have a dance."

All the people had to hear was the tuning of the fiddle and again we had a door yard full of people having a ball, it was important to have these kinds of gatherings and they all happened without a reason. It doesn't seem so long ago. In spite of what was going on we really made these get togethers special and we knew how to have fun which played a big role in our lives and helped us to survive.

Chic came out the door to join the festivities and asked mom,

"What was going on a while ago?"

Everyone started talking and papadad piped up and told Chic he thought it was raining.

Mom said, "Do we have to go all through this again?"

"Yes, because Chic wants to know what happened." Papadad said.

Now Chic was thoroughly confused. I started to laugh because they all looked confused. Everyone was talking at once and no one seemed to know what happened. Chic just stood there with her little clay pipe between her teeth and not removing it when she was talking and it bobbed up and down every time she said something. Everyone looked so silly especially to a little girl who didn't understand what they were talking about or trying to do. You had to be there. Dad had just gotten home from visiting with Johnny and Martha Green and he said to mom,

"I could hear you all laughing way down the lane."

This went on for quite a while and now mom had to explain to dad what had happened.

Dad said, "Dolly sure keeps us laughing."

Papadad agreed, "Shall we keep her?"

Everybody hollered, "Yes!" and clapped their hands. I was happy to belong to this family.

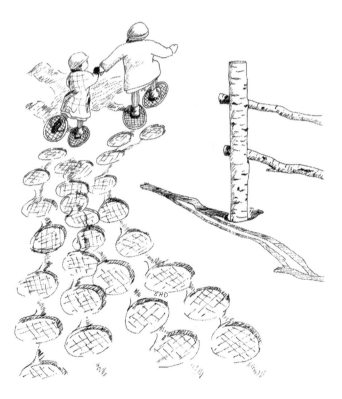

My Snowshoes

THE DATE WAS ABOUT NINETEEN THIRTY-SIX, I had gone with dad earlier in the year to get a whole lot of red willow whips. He chose them because he said they bend without breaking but I had no idea what he was going to do with them.

As time passed dad would be working with papadad out in the summer kitchen, we weren't allowed out there since it was too cold for us. Mom was busy making bean soup and fry bread for supper and we were helping. She said I could go play. I was standing by the front window with my head in my hands watching it snow. I wanted so much to go out and play but I didn't have a coat warm enough to wear outside. My two grandmothers and mom were busy sewing me a coat that was made from my Uncle Jim's pants. Chic was a good knitter; she had the job of knitting the lining for my coat. I never went out for a long time because it took them a long time to knit my coat. They also made a coat for Barb out of Uncle Nick's pants. They had bought us black rubber boots and we wore three pairs of socks. Finally they were finished with our coats and we were allowed to go out doors but not until we put on three pairs of long brown socks and these dark blue bloomers that Chic made.

The legs came down to our knees with elastic to keep the snow from getting our legs wet. We went out doors and our blue bloomers were sticking out from below our dress and coat, I sure didn't like these bloomers but they kept us warm. We even had a rabbit muff made from rabbits that dad trapped. Mom made rabbit stew from these same rabbits, nothing was ever wasted; she said that there was enough stew for everyone at Tyendinaga.

Not long after dad came out doors with papadad. He sat on a stump and I sat on his knee while dad tied these round objects to my feet, Barb had a pair too. The soles were made of dried animal gut. We were having a hard time trying to walk but we didn't sink in the snow, we kept falling because we couldn't get our feet close enough together. Dad was trying to explain to papadad what was going on. They both sat down on a stump and really laughed. Barb and I couldn't walk so we decided to run, this was also impossible.

We were out there a long time trying to manage these things that were tied to our feet, we thought we were being punished. We finally went in the house, our blue bloomers were all covered with different sizes of snow balls that mom was picking off and throwing out doors. We were about to have supper and Barb and I lay down on the floor on a quilt by the stove and went to sleep. Chic came in for supper along with Jakey and asked mom what was wrong with the girls and mom said they must be tired from being out doors in the snow all afternoon. Mom said she had never seen two little girls work so hard at anything, they wouldn't give up. We were trying to walk and run in the new snowshoes that papadad and dad had made. I never knew what they were called until the next day. We finally learned how to walk in them and it took nearly the whole winter, so now I could go and help dad get some wood in the bush. I remember wearing them down to the bay and trying to walk to Point Anne to see Chic. It was too far away so I decided to go back home.

I didn't know if anybody saw me out on the ice or not, it was still daylight when I went down there. I must have looked kind of tiny because I was quite a ways out before someone came to see where I was. I was already heading back home when I saw someone coming with a lantern. It turned out to be dad.

He asked me," Where were you going?"

I said," To see Chic."

"Gramma doesn't live there any more; she lives down on the Slash road."

I had no idea where that was. "Can we go there and see Chic?"

"Sure" said dad.

Dad never scolded me for being way out there on the ice. He knew I wouldn't do that again because Chic didn't live there any more. I recall us all going down on the Slash Road to visit with Chic. I don't know how long it was after I was out on the bay with my snow shoes on but dad kept his word. One day out of the blue dad hitched up our horse to the sleigh and we headed off to visit Chic. Dad heated up some stones and wrapped them in a blanket and laid them under the seat where he and mom were sitting and that's where Barb and I sat on some hay holding on to our youngest sister Carmel and covered up with blankets. I can't remember why we were going except I told mom I sure got lonesome to see Chic. Mom took some canned fruit and other food stuff when we left that day. When we arrived it was late in the day and dad carried Carmel into the house because she was asleep and uncle Ike picked Barbara and I up and put us on the ground and we were jumping around in the snow. Uncle Ike, my grandmother's brother helped dad unload the sleigh then they took the horse and sleigh out to the barn. I asked uncle Ike to lay the blanket over the horse's back to keep him warm.

The next day Chic was up early and so was I. We shared a cup of tea but mine was only make believe. Later on in the day mom's sisters all showed up with their families and they each had brought a lot of food. It turned out to be a midwinter ceremony. A lot of activity was taking place. Again it was very important that we as a family were able to be together. I learned a lot about our way of life in my young years and I thank my people forever for the things they taught such as caring, sharing and just being there for each other and of course our spirituality was always in the forefront and was very important to us in our everyday lives. This is really who we are; by holding these ceremonies and keeping them alive in us, we as Mohawk people are very fortunate to have such a rich culture. I am proud of my people. We had wonderful times living at the beach, it was my home. My roots will be there forever, in that special place called Tyendinaga.

My Grandfather Lewis

HIS NAME WAS PETER LEWIS BUT I called him papadad. He would sit on a stump in the door yard and play with my sister Barbara and I for hours and we played a lot of guessing games. He had a lot of patience and we had a lot of fun with him. He was a loving and kind papadad. Sometimes when he and dad weren't too busy and that wasn't very often, dad would bring out his fiddle and play a lot of toe tapping music. I'd go in the house and get papadad's spoons so he could play the music along with my dad. He was left handed so while sitting on the stump tapping his feet he always brought his left leg up quite high to keep time with the music. This event might take place in the afternoon. Before long people would show up rolling their own stumps down the laneway and they usually stayed until way after dark. They stopped playing music long enough to eat, this gave the people time to go home and get their food but they always brought it back with them and everybody ate together. After the music resumed papadad told Barbara and I to get up and dance because the frogs at the oopops pond heard the music and they started to sing and dance; so Barbara and I got up and danced, I would be step dancing and she would be just jumping up and down swinging her arm in every direction. Soon after that everyone got up and started dancing or jumping because they were doing what ever made them feel good. Some were just clapping their hands or singing like the frogs 'go 'round go 'round'.

I remember papadad asking me to take him up to the carrot patch to get some for our supper. He got down on his knees and me along with him to see what he was doing. He felt the top of the carrots to see how big they were to make sure it was big enough to eat. We picked a few and he asked me to open my apron so I could carry the carrots home. I would hold my apron with one hand and hang on papadad with the other. When we got home he would drop them in a pail of water to wash them then he would give them to mom. Sometimes we would go back to the carrot patch and pick two carrots, wipe the dirt off on his shirt and go for a walk chewing our carrots. He was always trying to teach me how to whistle and I told him I couldn't do that because I don't have any whiskers. I never did learn how to whistle so he taught me a little song and it goes like this;

Tweedle O Twill
Tweedle O Twill puffin' on corn silk
Tweedle O Twill whittling on wood
Sittin' here wishin' I could go fishin'
Over the hill Tweedle O Twill

I remembered the words and even the tune. I sang this song to my sister on the phone and I told her about this little song and she remembered it soon as I started singing, it was quite emotional and we both almost cried.

I love my papadad very much; we always had so much fun. He seemed to have time for us. As I look back now I know that all the time spent with him was exceptional. He was a very proud man.

Lying Corn

————〰●〰————

THE FALL SEASON CAME AROUND AND we all helped to gather our crops at this time, also dad bent the onions over and left them in the ground to dry for a while. The squash, turnips and potatoes were all dug up and prepared for storage. This is the time we shared with everyone who lived there so dad filled the wagon with vegetables and delivered some to every household. There also was fruit that was preserved for winter including wild blueberries, gooseberries that I never cared for, peaches elderberries and strawberries. We even had dried apples that mom cut into thick slices, placed them on a string and hung them on the wall behind the stove to dry. To lye the corn my mother would take a big pot and half fill it with water and added screened hardwood ashes and bring it to boil; after it boiled the white floured corn was added and cooked for days. The corn was cooked until it doubled in size and sometimes split. The part of the kernel that was attached to the cob would turn black and the rest had a yellowish colour. Before you could use it in soup it had to be washed several times in cold water until the water came clear.

When the corn was ready to shuck, Chic showed me how

to do that and she always had to start by rubbing two ears of dried corn together and the kernels dropped in a pail, we did this for a long time. I remember having sore fingers; the corn was something else we shared. When dad delivered the corn to the neighbours they thanked him and said,

"We don't mind shucking the corn ourselves."

Dad said, "That's okay it's all been done for you."

One of the neighbours had given dad some Indian beans and I asked mom,

"What kind of beans are they?"

"We have special beans that only Indians grow. They are at least three times bigger than normal beans." mom said.

I asked her, "Are we Indian?"

She said, "Oh yes, we have to be Indian to grow Indian beans." I have not forgotten.

Some of the corn was left on the cob and the husks were braided together and hung up in the summer kitchen to store while others were shucked and stored in big barrels so we had plenty of corn for the winter. Mom got together with a group of other women to start getting things for our thanksgiving ceremony; these meetings took weeks I'm sure. The children weren't in on any of this, we just played. Finally the day had come when they all decided what each one of them was going to do and they had all worked hard. The day we all had waited for was here at last.

"If it is a nice day we will have it down at the bay." Mom said.

The next day was beautiful and mom said, "It is Indian summer."

"Tell me what this is?" I asked, "What is Indian summer?"

"That's when Creator gives all Indian people some extra warm weather to get all their chores done that they have to do." Mom said.

We went down to the beach for the ceremony because there were too many people for anyone's house to accommodate. We all asked Creator to come and join us that day and every day; I couldn't recall whether he did or not then I remembered that my papadad told me if there are any leaves left on the trees and they are moving then Creator is present and the leaves were moving.

Dad had built a huge fire with stones all around the outside edge and special stones representing the four directions. This fire was used for keeping our food hot; the men had brought an old bed spring they laid on the fire to put our food on. I can't remember who all came but the people I do remember were uncle Jim, uncle Nick and Chic who landed on the shore in the boat as a special surprise. Mom's sisters, the Hills, Williams, Brants and more of the Lewis's all came to the gathering.

When it came time to eat mom asked papadad to thank Creator for our food and remember the ones who are sick and the ones who have changed places and not forgetting us. Then everyone shared in the food that was prepared by the people my mom's age. There was so much food I only remember what mom made; she had pea soup and Johnny cake and her special cottage cheese, it was really good stuff and my sister and I gorged ourselves on it. The elders were always served first out of respect; the children who were big enough to serve did so. When everyone was looked after and mom fixed my plate I went and stood beside papadad who I told,

"Grandmother Moon was looking at us, how come she was awake?"

"She got up early so she could come to the feast. Does she have a smile on her face?" he asked.

"Oh yes, a big, big smile." I said, "And she even winked at us."

Things went very well that day and most important we were all together again sharing in this ceremony. When everyone was finished eating we washed our plates off in the bay; mom put our plates in the wagon but before we all headed home dad said,

"Would anyone like to dance?"

"I would." I said. Then out came the fiddles and everyone had a whale of a time dancing on the old barn door. I was so surprised when I saw my grandmother and papadad round dancing, she seemed to be leading him and they were the only pair on the floor for a few minutes. What a wonderful day we had, one that I will never forget. At the beach where I grew up it will always hold special memories for me.

Looking For Freshwater Clams

THE BAY OF QUINTE WAS MADE famous by the aboriginal people who lived on its shores. I'm referring to all the wonderful and special times that were spent there by my people. When I was living there I knew that no other place existed.

My dad and I would go down to the bay every day to catch fish or sometimes freshwater clams. He and I waded out in the water quite a ways and he always had a pail with him. We walked out quite a ways to a piece of land that stretched out into the bay right off the end of Ridge Road. Dad and I walked all around the shore of this piece of land to find clams; most times we would find enough to fill a pail and sometimes we weren't so lucky. When we had enough in the pail we took them home and mom would wash and clean them and cook them in some milk with carrots and onions. We had them for our night time meal; I didn't like them but ate them anyway. Papadad would make it a fun time at this meal; he would put one of the clams in his mouth and make a noise like a croaking frog.

I asked him "What was that noise?"

"Oh Dolly, that's how the frogs ate there night meal."

Of course we would all be laughing. So along with all the

distraction I ate the clams and didn't even remember eating them. After we ate some of the neighbours stopped by just to visit and we would all be out doors. Mom made a big pot of tea steeped in a kettle, everyone had their own tin cup and the sun would be just going to bed over the bay.

I looked and watched the sun and told Chic "You don't live there any more."

Chic said "No, why dolly?"

"Because that's where Grandfather Sun lives now and he's having a wash in the bay before He goes to bed just like we do."

Chic smiled at me and said "Yes."

The time had come to get the fiddles and I was real happy. Dad gave papadad his fiddle first and he started tuning it up; everyone got up from where they were sitting, I guess they were waiting to dance. I happened to look up and saw Peter 'Boots' Williams coming across the field playing his mouth organ. Joker Brant and his wife dropped by and he had his spoons. I looked and coming through the hay field as he got closer I hollered "Here comes 'Black Snake Johnny' with his guitar."

Everyone started laughing. We had to wait until everyone stopped laughing at what I had said before they could start to dance. I recalled laughing too but I didn't remember why. Then Jakey came to join in or to see what was happening. Dad told everyone to step back and watch Jakey dance. They did but of course Jakey couldn't dance. Dad called him the left legged dancer. I danced a lot that time; we all had a wonderful time. That's what made it so special living at the Beach.

Papadad was blind so I told him "The trees were dancing also."

"What kind of dance were they doing?"

I said, "The sugar maple stomp."

He just kind of hummed; he asked me "Are you going to dance?"

I said "I just got finished."

He then said "Listen everyone, Dolly is going to dance for us to the "Sugar maple stomp".

Everyone clapped. After I danced I went and sat down on the grass to rest. I saw my mom who was rather a short lady get up on a stump and she said in Mohawk "Let's have a square dance."

People got up and began to dance. The fiddlers were superb. I recalled dad wore out a string on his fiddle, he kept on playing.

Someone remarked about the string "If Jakey could dance using his left leg then I could still play a three stringed fiddle.

Everyone said "Go for it Budge."

Papa dad said "It sounds much better."

I was watching with all the children and we were laughing because all we saw was legs and big feet. Chic danced by with her skinny legs and wrinkled up socks and I laughed louder. Everyone had a wonderful time; they must have danced all night. Now I saw Grandmother Moon making her way to the dance. These are very special times and I relive them quite frequently and so thankful I was there with my people at all these important times. I've learned well, I know the importance of all these things that I was involved with. I will forever remember. These things I've talked about are very important; they have to be brought forward. Mom made a big pan of Johnny cake and we had some while it was still warm. I can still see the maple syrup oozing out of the little holes in the cake when I put my fork in it to put a piece in my mouth.

Just writing about these events I can see all my people happy and carefree and can still taste the juices running down the inside of my mouth. We worked hard looking after ourselves and each other and had fun and good times.

Looking For The Cow's Cud

BARBARA AND I WERE ALWAYS LISTENING in on our elders talking. One day when we were living at Simon John's farm, we were listening in on their conversation when we heard my dad say that the cow had lost its cud and we had no idea what a cud was or what it looked like for that matter. Neither one of said anything to anyone. Can you imagine two little girls trying to find out what this thing was? I took Barbara by the hand and off we went in search of the cud. We went to the barn first and looked around where the cows had been standing and laying and saw nothing unusual. I thought if I don't know what it looks like how are we supposed to know when we find it. Barbara suggested we go see Bossy, she was our jersey cow. I agreed but said she would only say moo. We thought that something might happen to the cow if she wasn't able to find her cud. We looked at each other holding on hands and dancing and singing, "What is a cud, what is a cud? Maybe it's in her belly because we can't see it and she might not give us any more milk."

We didn't even know which cow had lost her cud and we couldn't tell by looking at them. We took turns looking in the cows ears with a flashlight. They looked at us kind of funny with big rolling eyes. Barbara and I thought we knew all about cows but this cud thing was a stumper.

Barbara asked me again, "What does it look like?"

I remember lifting up the cow's eyelid to see if it was ok. We both started crying thinking the cow would go blind.

"What would we do with a blind cow? We would have to get it some dark glasses like papadad wears."

So we began to look for something that looked like an eye. The both of us hunted all morning then we sat on a pile of hay beside the barn door but we never found it. We didn't want our cow to have to go to bed without a cud. We didn't want to ask dad because we wanted to surprise him by finding her cud but we didn't find it that day. We both woke up early the next morning and the first thing we did was to run to the barn to see if the cows were ok. They were standing there eating some hay. We both headed to the hay field. While we were down in the lower field dad asked mom,

"What are the girls doing?"

Mom said, "They are looking for the cow's cud, they asked me if they could go and try and find it, and I said yes; they have been looking since yesterday."

Mom said, "We should tell the girls that the cow got her cud back. We should make them believe that they helped the cow find her cud."

Dad said "Okay we can do that by telling them that they cared so much for the cow and Bossy knew they were upset because of what happened."

He told us "It is something the creator gave the cow to keep forever." He wasn't sure either what it looked like or at least he wouldn't tell us.

"Does the cud make the cow happy like you are when you play your fiddle?" I asked.

I look back at that time in my life and smile with pleasure, what wonderful times I had. I did find out in later life how she lost her cud and where it went. To this day I still marvel how patient, loving and understanding my whole family was and how important it was to have each other.

Grandma Rose Lewis

———➤●◄———

ON THE TWENTY SEVENTH OF APRIL eighteen eighty nine my grandmother Rose Brant married my grandfather Peter Lewis at Tyendinaga. She was always busy; she was the knitter in our family and would get all kinds of wool from the neighbours. Sometimes we all had to help by unraveling things that had been already made and had big heaps of wool on the floor. When it came time to tie the ends of the wool together grandma would fix them so you would never know they were separated. She would make us all mittens, colourful socks, hats and sweaters. She was making papadad a sweater out of khaki wool, the back was finished and she told me she was going to put raglan sleeves in it which I didn't know what that was at the time so she said she would show me when it was finished. The sweater finally got finished and papadad modeled it for us; it had great big shiny brass buttons that I wondered why they were so big and it turned out that it was easier for him to do up his sweater. Papadad said to Rose that if he ever fell down on his belly he would never get up. After he modeled his sweater grandma laid it on the table and began to explain to me about the raglan sleeve; the front and back of the sweater was knitted closer together as she finished it off at the neck. The two sleeves were knitted in the shape of a vee which fitted perfectly when they were sewn together. I asked him if I could try on the sweater and he said let grandma help you. When I put on the sweater part of it was lying on the floor and so were the sleeves and I said it looked a lot better on papadad. One time when I was standing behind her watching her knit and she asked me to bring some of the wool from the pile to her feet; she wanted to knit after supper. Well as things happen we had forgotten to buy coal oil for the lamp so dad went to Shannonville to get some and I went with him. We were having some trouble, we couldn't find any place open and the person who would trade with dad sometimes wasn't home. I know dad was upset so we stopped at a neighbours on the way home and he gave us enough for the night. When we got back home grandma said,

"Where did you go for the coal oil, you've been gone all night?"

Dad felt he had to explain to everyone what had happened. Grandma sat in her rocking chair, took two needles and a piece of wool and put a few stitches on them and asked me,

"Would you like to learn how to knit?"

I'm left handed and grandma was trying so hard to teach me to knit and papadad had made me some knitting needles,

"These aren't to play with." he said.

She resumed showing me how to knit but she was having a terrible time and she gave up. "Let Chic teach you when she comes to visit." she said.

A few days later Chic came for a visit and grandma asked her to show me how to knit. She stood behind me and managed to teach me a few stitches. I was knitting on this for a long time and it was a little long and she asked me,

"What are you going to do with it?"

I said, "It's going to be a scarf for my sock doll."

I wasn't allowed to knit during the day since I had chores to do and had some playing to do too. I caught on to knitting pretty well and when Chic came to visit I'd show her what I was making. After a long time had passed I graduated from two needles to four and was making socks.

Chic decided she didn't have to help me any more. I guess I was very determined to finish this sock as I was sitting beside the stove sweating and brushing the hair out of my eyes and mom was telling me how to take the stitches off the needle. Gram was really pleased with my progress, she asked me to show papadad so I took my sock over and put it in his hand and he said,

"These are going to be warm." As he put his hand in the sock he told me,

"It had no heel."

I misunderstood and thought he said it had no eel and I couldn't figure out what he was talking about.

"I'm not making socks for the eel."

He said "No, no Dolly, I said it doesn't have a heel." He and I had a good laugh. I made a sock to match. I made many more socks after that and none of them ever had heels in them, you could put them on any which way you wanted.

My uncle Nick was over seas in the army and I had no idea where that was, I asked Chic,

"Was uncle Nick mad at us?"

"No." she said with tears in her eyes.

"I'm sorry I made you cry."

She was lonesome for her son and I'm sure she had a lot of sleepless nights. I made my uncle a scarf and we each sent him over a chocolate bar. When my uncle Nick was lucky enough to come home from the war he wasn't allowed to go visit his mother on the reserve and when he did he had to sneak and get there by night as not to get caught. He even lost his status. To my understanding there were a great many aboriginal people treated the same way. Uncle Nick told me the scarf was warm and it was long enough to wrap around his neck about four times.

Gathering Elderberries

MY GRANDMOTHER'S NAME WAS MARGARET ELLEN Green and she was my mother's mother and we were always together. I recall one time we were walking down the road hanging on hands when we met someone who asked,

"Are you two joined at the hip?"

I asked Chic "What is a hip?"

She said "Never mind, I'll tell you later."

I'm not sure where we were going but only that we were on our way to gather some elderberries. We walked for quite a ways and we went either down by the bay or across from where the ceremony is held for the Mohawk Landing. I talked this over with my mom before she changed places and she was surprised that I could remember because I was only four years old. She didn't know where we went since she didn't go with us. There seemed to be a lot of places where they grew. Before we came upon the elderberry bushes we sat down somewhere by the river where Chic made us a cup from a piece of birch bark then she laid down on her belly and got each of us a drink of water. She had also brought some buttermilk biscuits she carried in her apron for us to have a snack. We rested there for a while before we carried on and I was running around playing when I got caught up in some tall grass and fell down. Just then we saw something.

I asked Chic, "What is that?"

She told me, "Be quiet."

I sat down on her lap and she whispered to me what it was. I knew when anyone whispered I was supposed to be quiet.

"It's a raccoon, you must have scared it when you fell down."

"What is it doing?" I asked.

She said, "He's fishing like dad does."

I said "Yes, but he doesn't have a pole."

We both laughed silently and I whispered, "He would look funny with a fish pole."

"This is one of Creator's children." she said, "and we aren't supposed to ever hurt any of these animals that we are seeing. See his eyes; it looks like he has glasses on."

I said "Like papadad in a way. Look! He's washing his food like mom does; he's a lot like us isn't he?"

He finally walked out of the water from where he was fishing up onto the bank. He looked our way and Chic was talking to him in Mohawk. She told him I was her baby and it was the first time I had ever seen him, she thinks you're beautiful and will always remember what you look like and then he ran off in the bush. We resumed walking again and it wasn't long and we were at the elderberry bushes. They looked like little blue umbrellas hanging from the branches. We were there for a long time picking them.

"Why are they called elderberries?" I asked while holding her hands and looking at her with my head to one side.

She said, "Just a minute and I'll show you."

She reached up and picked one berry, laid it in her hand and said, "Look, it's got wrinkles like grandma." We both had a big laugh.

Chic had two big pails and I had a one little one and we were able to fill all of them before we headed back home. We went back home the same way we got there even stopping to get another drink and I carried the birch bark cup in my apron pocket. We finally arrived home and everyone was happy to see us. Mom told Chic,

"Dad was getting a little anxious because we were late getting home but everything is okay now."

Everything we ever did we never just did it, there was always an adventure in whatever we were doing. We even had the most important letter from the Indian agent that I carried in my shoe. You never really knew when he would show up. For all the atrocities we went through I know they were trying to break us. For me it has made me a much stronger person and more determined to beat them at their own game. They will never have another opportunity to do that again. We will all have to pull together to be a stronger nation and I believe we can make it happen. I read our great law quite often; this is where I get my strength and determination, we don't need all these other things cluttering up our lives. We have to break the cycle, get involved and talk to each other more often.

Living At Simon John's Farm

WE LIVED AT SIMON JOHN'S FARM that dad had taken over and farmed when we were all quite small. We had three cows, one pig, some chickens and of course one bad rooster. We had a large garden where we grew corn, squash, beans and other vegetables along with a huge patch of rhubarb. The leaves were quite large; I remember playing in the rhubarb patch and pretending I was lost in the bush. Then I would call my sister to come find me. When Chic came by and tried to find us we could see her coming and we laid down on the ground and started to giggle because we were looking at her little skinny legs and wrinkly socks coming through the rhubarb patch. Sometimes my uncle Ike, Chic's brother, would be visiting us so he would come and look for us also while he was whistling and singing silly songs like 'She'll be coming 'round the mountain'. We would be just squirming while lying on the ground laughing so hard. At this time I would try to whistle and they would find us.

We played for a little while then Chic said "It's time to go back to work."

Our job was to help pick weeds from the vegetable garden and we always had to do our chores for a certain length of time before we were allowed to play.

One day Barbara and I were playing at the side of the house facing the sun where there happened to be an old broken down fence with rusty old wires growing in the side of a big old maple tree. On the fence stretching a long ways into the field there were thousands of little green egg shaped objects with burrs on them. We didn't know what they were so we picked some and put them in our apron to take them in the house to ask mom what they were.

Mom said "These are wild cucumbers, you can play with them but you must not eat them."

Barb and I started throwing them at each other and they got stuck in our hair and it took mom two days to get them out of our hair with bear grease. I asked dad if he could get the wire fence from the tree. I remember helping him; when the fence was removed I helped dad tie a big white cloth on the tree to help it heal.

Chic came by to visit and said to mom "When I was walking up the road I saw a big rag tied on the tree, what's it for?" Mom told her what it was for.

Chic said "I think Dolly's a very caring person."

Mom said "I know, I hope she won't grow out of it."

They both discussed what kind of child I was and decided that's the way I was and nothing could be done about it.

Chic lived on the York Road just up the hill towards Shannonville where the school house once stood and I was able to visit her every day. I walked through the cow pasture when I went to visit her. I was on my way to Chic's just starting through the pasture when a person came with two horses and a wagon to pick up the milk that dad had left out by the road. I don't know if dad was ever paid for the milk or not.

I was standing by the milk stand and I asked this person "Do you want some eggs, we have lots of eggs."

He laughed and said "Not today."

The family of Iva Lewis lived in the same area, I remember Iva better than the rest. This time mom filled the honey pail full of cream and I was told to deliver it to Iva Lewis' house. I could stay and visit for a while and Iva would bring me back home. She would sometimes pick me up and carry me. I wanted to play along the way home and she was in a hurry. She was telling me who the people were that lived around that area but I can't remember their names now.

I recall asking her "How far are we from the beach?"

She asked me "Why?"

I told her "I missed playing in the water and I liked it better being there and I like the other house better."

She told me "Talk to mom about that. I miss being there too."

"Why, did you live there? I don't remember seeing you at the beach."

She said "No, but I used to go down there quite often."

"Do you remember seeing me down there step dancing?"

Iva said "No but I know you can dance pretty well. Who showed you how to dance?"

I said "Nobody, I just did it."

She said "Well we are nearly home again from our little trip."

"What's a trip?" I asked.

"It means a visit with me."

I said "Okay."

We stopped on the Slash Road so she could light her lantern then we carried on walking she hanging on my hand. Dad was coming down the lane way to meet us with the lantern. I hugged her goodnight, let go of her hand and ran to meet dad. Mom was waiting for me in the open door with my two sisters. My sisters and I hugged; I kissed my mom and told her I loved her. She gave me a dish of fresh strawberries and I went to bed.

Dad hollered at mom and told her "I'm walking Iva half way home."

Mom said "Okay and thanks to Iva."

I had a busy day. This is how we spent some of our time. I had a lot of fun but I don't know if anyone else did or not. She would say goodnight and leave to go back home. This running back and forth went on all summer. Everyone always visited back and forth all the time and they seemed to have a lot of fun when they were all together.

Missing My Papadad

—⟫●⟨—

I WILL ALWAYS REMEMBER PLAYING AND having a lot of fun with my papadad. He was gentle and a very soft spoken person and very loving. We would play all sorts of games and go for long walks while hanging on his little finger and he told me a lot of stories that I'm passing on to our children.

He was blind as I have mentioned before but again I never knew what this was and I didn't realize until I was older that he could not see. He could play the fiddle just like my dad. He would also try to step dance with me but he couldn't so everyone would laugh and I would just keep on dancing. I recall him offering to help my dad as often as he could. He and dad and I would go down to the beach with a home made wagon to get some wood so we could have a fire all night. Dad took the axe and he tried to chop an old partly dead willow tree up to fit in the wagon. In the meantime papadad was sitting on a stump waiting for dad to chop enough wood to fill the wagon.

Papadad must have sat there for a long time because he asked dad "Why is there no wood in the wagon?"

Dad said "This tree must be made of iron, I can't make a notch in it with the axe, and it just keeps bouncing off the wood."

Papadad laughed and told dad "You will never be able to chop this wood because of the kind of tree it is."

So dad went home and got the saw. It was a long time after we got the wood from the bay when papadad got sick with a bad cold and grandma and mom kept putting mustard plasters on his chest and feet and the reason the plasters were on his feet is because that is where all illnesses leaves the body especially the cold. I can't remember how long he was sick.

I don't remember papadad being sick before. He used to get up early in the morning and I could hear him and down stairs I would come. We always had a little chat. He would ask me if I had a good nights sleep.

I would say "Yup, did you?"

He'd laugh and say "Yes."

This one time I got up early and I didn't hear him downstairs, mom was the only one home.

"Where is everybody?" I asked.

Mom said "Dad and grandma were gone somewhere."

I asked "Where did they go?"

She said "Papadad doesn't feel well."

I went in the bedroom and checked and he was lying in bed covered up to his neck.

I said "He's okay."

Mom says "Grandma and dad will be back soon."

I guess I was happy then because I went out to play. It wasn't long after I checked in on papadad that grandma and dad got back home and this time mom asked us girls to go and play with Joker Brant's kids. We were gone for a long time. When we went back home papadad was gone.

I asked everyone "Where is papadad?"

They said "He went to see someone in Shannonville."

I said "Why didn't he take me?"

"It will be too late for you to stay up."

"Will he be home tomorrow?"

Grandma said "Yes."

I didn't really know or understand why papadad wasn't home just that I knew he went somewhere without me and I thought he was playing hide and seek with me. I tried so hard to find him; I looked in the potato patch and corn patch and couldn't find him anywhere. I remember going to the beach and looking behind the big willow tree and calling him and I was crying telling him I loved him and to come home with me for supper because "I know how much you love corn soup and fry bread." I couldn't find him anywhere.

"Papadad, you know you can't see and you shouldn't be out here alone, you might get lost."

It was very difficult for me being so young and not understanding what was going on. I remember grandma giving me papadad's cap to wear hoping it would help me not to miss him so much. I didn't know what was wrong or what had happened. I recall dad picking me up with tears in his eyes and showing me papadad.

I remember kissing him on the cheek and asking him "Why are you sleeping in that funny bed?" I told him "It was time to get up now; we are supposed to be going for a walk."

Papadad went to the spirit world in nineteen thirty eight and he was buried at Tyendinaga.

I really had a good relationship with my papadad. When we would go for long walks for instance, we would talk about just anything. He would always listen to what I was saying. One day when we were walking down the road holding on hands I remember telling him this is where we picked the apples. He was being silly that day making me laugh and he was whistling funny tunes.

He said "Listen, can you whistle?"

I said "No 'cause I don't have any mustache."

He laughed so hard he bent right over front wards.

"Do I have to learn how to do that?"

"No, but when you do know how to whistle you will know that I will be walking beside you and that you will be thinking of me."

Well papadad, I'm all grown up now and a mother and grandmother, I never learned to whistle and I do think of you all the time and I love you every day and when I am walking you are beside me. If I listen really carefully I can hear your voice talking to me and we are even laughing. That's some of the silly things that happened to us; like when your cap fell in the ditch. I'll always cherish these special time and memories I have of those long ago years. You were a wonderful papadad and a silly one to boot.

Garter Snake

————➤●◄————

I WAS ABOUT FIVE YEARS OLD and my sister and I were always together. She was afraid of creepy worms in particularly the kind that makes nests up in the bushes. This day we were playing outside and we wandered over towards the corn field where there were other vegetables growing, I was walking ahead of her on the path when I stepped off the path for a few steps because I had spotted a few garter snakes wriggling along the path then they slithered off into the long grass. I probably scared them. I kept on walking but never said a word. We played there for quite a while with our sock doll that Chic had made for us from a pair of old socks that uncle Jim had worn. They had yarn hair and big black button eyes. It must have been noon because we saw Peter 'Boots' Williams walking along the edge of the bush which he did every day at the same time on his way to the village. That's how I could tell it was twelve o'clock. He wore rubber boots every day and in all seasons, they were black to his knees with red soles which the toe part came right up over the front of his foot. He was a small person and he lived with his mother in the same area where we lived. We were all good neighbours that lived in this part of the Mohawk community. We headed back to the house for something to eat. After we had eaten we went back outside to play. Some time along in the afternoon Chic, papadad and grandma were all sitting on stumps having a puff on their little clay pipes. Chic had been sitting there for some time in the warm sun and then dozed off with her pipe quivering between her teeth. Mom was always telling Chic to pull up her socks so I decided to tie a snake around her knee because it was called a garter snake and I guess I thought it would hold up her socks. It took a little while before she woke up and in the meantime the snake which I tied around her knee was enjoying the warm sun too. As I sat there watching, the snake began to move, Chic stirred, looked down at her lap and saw her dress moving. She picked up her dress above her knee and saw the snake around her leg and began hollering, jumping up and down and dancing. I really didn't know what was going on and boy could she ever dance without a fiddle playing. My papadad was blind and asked mom what happened. Mom told him that I had tied a small snake around chic's knee to keep up her sock. Papadad said think about it, she's smart to come up with that idea. Chic calmed down after a bit and I made everyone laugh again that day. Chic never got mad at me for what I had done so I guess it was all right with everyone. I was always doing something, always had lots of fun. What ever happened I made sure everyone was involved. I was only trying to have fun and make everyone happy. I remember the time I had with my whole family. Now that I'm all grown up and am a mom and grandmother and the love I have for my grandchildren, I have the knowledge and understanding of what it was like being Chic. She was a very loving and kind lady and I told her so every day and I still do.

Gathering Hickory Nuts

———>✦◆✦<———

I CAN'T REMEMBER WHAT YEAR IT was but we were living at Tyendinaga. We always walked through the swamp east of where Pete Williams lived with his mother and sister. After we got through the bush we came out on the York Road southeast of the cheese factory, which was on the Slash Road at that time. This event dad had our letter from the Indian agent. Our whole family walked down the York Rd. until we came to a place where the older people could sit down and rest across the road from the powwow grounds. There wasn't much open land here because it was all covered with hickory trees all the way to the bay shore and people called this place hickory nut grove. This tree is called a shagbark hickory and the nuts it produces are encased in a thick outer skin; as the skin dries it begins to split and inside is a small off white nut called a hickory nut. These nuts are good to eat and can be used for baking; mom would make a hickory nut cake for special occasions and this could well have been one of those occasions. We always met other people there but I can't remember who they were. By the time we arrived at hickory nut grove we were all tired and the children lay down in the long grass. The older people were stamping down the long grass to make a place where they could sit. In among the tall grass was some sweet grass which smelled like vanilla. Barb and I remember asking mom if we could chew on some and she said no but she managed to cut some and take a bundle home with her. Each mother and grandmother had enough food done up in a bundle for their families and we all ate together. Before we ate my dad and some of the other men would dig a hole in the ground and laid four rocks at the edge of the hole to represent the four directions. I was watching what they were doing and I asked my dad about all these things that were going on. He squatted down and told me why he was doing all this, I didn't really understand but I did remember. Dad brought some good wood from home that he tied in a bundle and carried on his back to make our sacred fire. We took a little time to eat and play and the elders would smoke their little white clay pipes, I can remember from looking at them that they all seemed very relaxed. When our eating time was all over and the people had rested, the mothers and grandmothers would put the rest of the food they brought wrapped neatly in bundles and laid all the bundles on a tall bush. I guess they didn't want the food lying on the ground where the animals could get it. After we gathered our hickory nuts we left them laying on the ground in a big pile then we all joined hands and it became a big circle and we were all chanting. This was the only time that my dad would bring his fife and played it at this ceremony. I remember trying to dance and my mom would squeeze my hand, I would look up at her and she would shake her head. I know now I was supposed to stop trying to dance and I did. My papadad would again thank Creator for this beautiful harvest and for all the people who shared the ceremony. We had a wonderful time and a memorable ceremony and I thank my father and my papadad for making me aware of these times and us all being together. Hope you will find as much pleasure in these ceremonies as I did. I am passing them on to you to share with the rest of our people.

Going For Groceries

It would always be in the evening when we would go to Shannonville for groceries because we wanted to avoid conflict with the white population. After we got our groceries we had to carry them back to where dad had hid the wagon. My youngest sister, Carmel, was hanging on mom's hand since she couldn't walk very fast as she was too little. When we got to where the wagon was dad put the groceries in the wagon and left a small place for Carmel to sit then we headed home. Mom was carrying the lantern, Barb was walking beside her and I was trying to help dad pull the wagon. We came to an area on our way where it was always damp and of course there was quite a lot of mosquitoes breeding and along with the mosquitoes were a lot of fireflies. Carmel told dad to hurry up and run because the mosquitoes were coming after all of us with lanterns and dad and I ran down the road a little ways just to keep her quiet. Dad was also carrying a bag of potatoes on his back and somehow the end of the bag came undone and potatoes were dropping all over the road. Mom, Barb and I had to pick up all the potatoes that had dropped. The next day mom cooked all the potatoes that had dropped because they were badly bruised. She made soup, potatoes pancakes, fried potatoes, potato patties, we had potatoes every meal. Dad liked the idea because he loved potatoes but papadad was getting rather sick of it,

"If we don't eat something different soon we will all look like a potato."

Barb and I laughed so hard our bellies were sore. Mom took some of the pancakes and gave them to the neighbours. One neighbor said,

"Thank you, Kathleen and you even cooked them."

The next time they saw mom they said the pancakes were really good. Mom just smiled,

"You should know by now all Indian women are good cooks."

This is one of those times we went to get groceries without a letter from the Indian agent. Most people did what they had to do with or without the letter. If we had waited for the government to give us permission without the letter we would have all perished. My hat goes off to all my people who took the bull by the horns and did what we had to do to survive and I'm glad they did. I came out of this time in my life living under pressure that the European people brought upon us and it has made me a stronger person. As I look back things could have been a lot better for us. I'm a residential school survivor. The things that happened haven't really gone away. I did have a wonderful life with my family in spite of it all; somehow we have to break the cycle because it's like being in a bad relationship and there is no one there to listen or to help and we can't go anywhere to escape it.

Gone Fishing

WHEN I WAS A LITTLE GIRL I lived at a place called Mohawk Beach on first nation's territory in Tyendinaga with my family. One day my dad took me fishing at Jakey's bridge which was about a quarter mile from home. We walked along the old railroad bed that had been there long before I was born. I never really knew what it was used for and I hadn't bothered to ask. The tracks had been removed so the railway bed and ties were left there for some unknown reason. My dad wouldn't let me get to close to the bridge since he didn't want me to fall in the river because neither one of us could swim. I was about six years old. Our fishing poles were made of poplar saplings and the lines were string and the hooks were made from a safety pin that dad had bent in the shape of a hook and it all worked just fine. Dad put my line in the water and gave it to me to hold then he put his in the water and we both sat down beside each other. We sat there for a little while; he was whistling little tunes and telling me stories. All of a sudden I felt a jerk on my line.

"Dad! I've got a bite!"

He said "Okay!" But he didn't bother to go and check it out. He was just sitting there with his legs crossed humming a tune. I asked him over and over to see what I had on my line but he paid no attention. I finally got up and jerked the line from the water and what ever it was flew and hit my dad right in the lap; that's all it took. Dad took one look and he was gone, running at a dead heat right back up the tracks in the opposite direction from the way we came and me right after him with my pole flung over my shoulder and hanging on to what ever I had for dear life. As I watched dad running up the tracks he had his pants rolled to his knees and we were both bare foot and he had really bowed legs. I can't explain it any better but I can still see him now. While he was running with me chasing, I was hollering,

"What is this I have on my line?"

But he never looked back, just kept running. He ran up our laneway past our house, past my mom who was standing in the door yard and was heading towards Johnny Greens house. When I got to where mom was I was all out of breath and I asked her,

"Have you seen dad?"

"Yes, he went by here with his head back and pants rolled up to his knees and arms flying in every direction; reminded me of the comic strip 'L'il' Abner.'

Mom asked "What have you got on your line?"

"I don't know." I said.

Just then Jakey came around the corner of the house and began to tell mom what he saw.

"I saw everything with Gord running up the tracks and Margaret in hot pursuit. What ever she was dragging on her line kept bouncing up and down on the ties. "Of course when I got home there was no skin left on this thing but they decided it was an eel. Jakey said

"My goodness that's a nice size eel."

"Do you want it?" mom asked Jakey. He declined.

"We'll bury it in the garden then; it will make good fertilizer." Mom said.

I didn't know that my dad was afraid of eels. As I looked down the path towards Greens I saw my dad coming home and ran to meet him. He stopped dead in his tracks. I told dad it was dead and buried in the garden and that's when he told me he didn't much care for those things. I guess he thought I still had the eel with me. We all gathered around in the door yard and my papadad and grandma came outside whom by now knew what had happened. We all had a good laugh at my dad's expense. I can still see my dad running and me chasing him and it still brings a smile to my face. Dad and I still went fishing quite often in the same place but he always stayed a fair distance from me; I haven't caught an eel since then.

All Dressed Up

A FEW YEARS AGO WHEN WE were young and living at the beach my sister Barbara and I would often get all dressed up in some old clothes that were much too big for us. Aunt Phyllis, dad's youngest sister, would dress us up in these clothes. She even put coloured bands of cloth around our heads. We would be dressed like this all day. We each had a little chair that dad had made for us and that's the only time I remember sitting in a chair because at our house only the older people were allowed to sit on a chair. I remember standing up while we were eating. Barb and I would drag our little chairs out towards the corn field. We had a small patch of earth that dad didn't plant anything in that was our play area. I recall that not too far from our play patch that grandma Rose had planted some flowers and she guarded them closely. They were growing up along the south side of the house and of course we got in a lot of trouble because we never planted anything we couldn't eat. Dad even got upset because she spent the money on flower seeds. Barbara and I would wander over to where these flowers were growing trying to find out what they were. Just then grandma would come outdoors and she would shoo us away. We thought she was playing with us. Every time she came outdoors we would run away, when she went back in the house we would sneak back up to the flower bed, and we would repeat our performance every time she would go in and out of the house. It took us a long time to figure out she didn't want us there. I'm sure that these episodes went on all summer, it was really bothering us because we weren't allowed to touch or smell them.

One day grandma was sitting outdoors in the sun by her flowers and I asked her

"Do you want me to get you a cup of tea and your pipe?"

She said "Okay, is Chic here yet."

I said "No, can Barbara and I have a cup of tea with you?"

"Sure, did you and Barbara get all dressed up just to have tea with grandma?"

I said "Yes, do you like our dresses?"

She said "Yes, did you know that is the kind of dresses that I wore when I was a little girl?"

"Were they too big for you too?"

She just smiled.

"Did you walk like this grandma?"

Grandma said "I don't know, show me how you walk."

So Barbara and I held each others arm and we picked up our dresses between our index finger and our thumb and our little finger was pointing out. Grandma smiled and said "How nice and happy you look like two little angels".

Grandma smiled and asked "Where is my tea?"

"I'll go right now and fetch it to you."

When I gave her the tea I asked "What are those things you don't want us to touch?"

She said "Come and I'll show you."

She told us they were flowers. "I planted them to make things look pretty."

I said "Like us?"

She just smiled and put her arm around the both of us.

"What are they called?"

"These are called cosmos." she said as she pointed to them. "The other ones are called pink hollyhocks."

We were satisfied with what she told us because we never went by them again. Grandma Rose was different than Chic, she was a more serious person about things but everything balanced itself out. She smoked a little white clay pipe but she never let me have a puff. She was a good grandma, she taught us to always be careful and always do what mom and dad tells us and always love each other. We loved her and we miss her.

These dresses we wore belonged to Aunt Phyllis. She always liked dressing Barbara and me up. Sometimes she would spend all day sewing some special thing on the dresses to make them prettier. We enjoyed these special times when we did this and I'm sure we went to many make believe places but really nowhere in particular only at the beach. I can honestly say that I have never had these flowers in my garden when I grew up because they hold bad memories. I loved my grandma but I felt the flowers took precedence over her grandchildren. She had these flowers and I know she enjoyed them because she grew them every year after that. We would never go around on that side of the house unless grandma was outside sitting by her flowers. My two grandmothers were very good friends. I remember them chatting away in Mohawk while my sister and I were sitting under the table listening to them. I remember a few words they said but Barbara didn't. They talked a while then they would be silent then they both laughed really hard for a long time and talked while they were laughing and we'd laugh right along with them but didn't know why. Grandma Rose never liked walking too much, she was quite content to sit and knit and sew; she was always making something. Chic and I did all the walking. We gathered baskets of hickory nuts and elder berries and other things for our food supply and we always shared with Chic. She would take some of the things we gathered home with her to Point Anne. I miss those times of gathering and the special relationship I had with both my grandmothers. My husband and I took a drive to Point Anne once when we were visiting because I wanted him to see the house where I was born but the only thing remaining was the cement stoop where I would sit and play with Chic. I still recalled what the house looked like inside and it was quite emotional for me but I had good feelings and I even had a flashback.

Dad's Trap Line

I DIDN'T HAVE A BROTHER SO when I was seven my dad took me along with him on his trap lines. It wasn't because I was helping, I'm sure it was because dad was lonesome. We would snowshoe to a few spots where quite often we got a beaver or a muskrat and I always watched dad take the animal out of the trap. This would be some of our food source. We rested for a while and dad made a small fire then packed snow in a can to be used to make tea. After the tea was made we always had a piece of fry bread that mom had given us, it tasted a lot different when you ate it in the bush. We had to visit three or four more trap sets to see if we had any more animals. We weren't too lucky that day, dad only caught two beaver. He always dressed them before we took them home. After this was done he and I got down on our knees and he held my hand as he whispered over the animal. I never said a word only listened; dad thanked me for being quiet. We stood up and dad asked me,

"Do you want to ask me any questions?"

"I didn't know what you were doing over the animal."

He said, "When you get an animal or anything you can eat, you always thank Creator for giving you this animal so you can survive and always thank the animal for giving its life. Now we have to give the animal back its spirit."

My grandmother Rose would make ceremonial rattles from the beaver's tail. She would put dried corn in the rattle she made after the tail was good and dry. My dad always stretched the pelt on a large oval shaped board with a hole in it for his finger and I was watching everything he was doing. The pelt would be put on the board inside out so the flesh side would dry. He gave mom the beavers and told her that Margaret was interested in what he was doing and did she think it was time that I learned how to clean the animal.

Grandma told mom, "This would be a good idea; we'll make an Indian out of her yet."

Papadad said, "I thought she was all ready."

I imagine dad got a bit of money for his pelts but I don't remember him having a lot of them. He enjoyed what he was doing and he was a very proud man. He and mom always managed to have food on the table for us. He taught me a lot of good things about our culture and particularly our spirituality. He taught me how to be brave and to always walk away when things weren't right which I've done all my life and I will always remember his teachings and I will always love my dad.

Fishing For Pickerel

After my papadad died in nineteen thirty eight we moved from our home at the beach to Shannonville. We rented a big house made of wide boards situated on the north side of Young Street in the fifth house from York Road. Just down the street was that mission school that I hated so much. I didn't like living in Shannonville; I found the people, unlike those who lived at the beach, very unfriendly and down right mean. I recall Chic living in the other half of this house. We didn't have as much fun living there. I don't ever remember people not being able to fish but this happened to us on the banks of the Salmon River that ran through Shannonville and passed right by the house where we were living. We had been going down to the river a lot to fish, I remember a lot of other people fishing there too. Some even went at night, we saw their lanterns and dad said it was easier to see the fish and where they were but we always fished during the day.

In nineteen forty we were fishing in the river west of the bridge one evening after supper. My dad, Uncle Ike, Uncle Nick my mom and us three girls were all down at the river fishing for pickerel. From what I remember and understand there had been a few unpleasant acts against us by some of the neighbours. Dad was fishing with a net which was legal and we all used it and had some fish on the river bank. We were all sitting there in a relaxed mood when I looked up and coming towards us on the path along the river was two men dressed in blue uniforms. As they got closer I told mom that they had guns at their side. They both started hollering at my dad hitting him and knocking him to the ground.

They were swearing at us and asked us "What in hell are you doing?"

Dad never said a word and neither did anyone else. I didn't know who they were or what they were doing there I only remember them being awful people, then one of the men started pushing my dad again. This was the same kind of treatment I received at school and I wondered what was wrong with them. Mom told them to leave dad alone and watch their language because there were little girls present. They hit her and she fell to the ground. I remember screaming at these people and hitting at them and told them to leave my parents alone. We three girls were all huddled together with our mom and dad and crying real hard. My two uncles couldn't help, they were told to stay out of it. I recall they had guns pointed at them. My dad was bruised quite badly and could hardly walk for a long time and he told us his hips were hurting where they had kicked him. It was a scary place for a while, I really thought they were going to shoot us and we were afraid. They were there for quite a while hitting their clubs against a tree and kicking at the grass. I guess they were mad. Finally one of them picked up the fish and put them in a sack They took dad's net and broke it and took all the rest of our stuff then left. My two uncles bent down and helped my mom get up, and she said "I've got a sore shoulder." We walked up the hill. That's the first time in my life that I saw my mom, dad and my uncles crying. When we got to the house I hugged dad and told him I loved him and everything would be okay. Mom was not able to do any cooking or house work or looking after us kids for quite a while and she cried a lot. Chic helped in the meantime. We also were having a hard time sleeping due to bad dreams. It was quite a while after that that I would go fishing.

I kept looking around for some more of these people to come back and beat the rest of us up. These people had no shame for what they did and certainly didn't care whether or not we had any food. Things haven't changed much. The people who are in power like all areas of government right down to the people who came to this land are still treating my people the same way. The police are still killing us and getting away with it. The hatred and racism are running this country and in the same breath it's such a wonderful place to live. I guess it is if you are not an aboriginal. There are so many things not right with us, like owning up to the truth about residential schools and the inhumane treatment that went on. I could keep going on about all the atrocities that were brought upon my people. We really have to find a way to break the bondage and be free by never being ruled by people in authority. I will always remember these racist remarks and actions. This is not the way we should be living.

Treatment of my people hasn't gotten any better over the years. As I grow older I have a deep love for my people; I don't know whether or not these things will ever change. We really have to find the road to freedom. I've heard that freedom costs, I am sure my people and I have paid dearly for that cost. For instance how can a Government give to a people what they already own? Land claims should never be a court issue. We were not represented in the courts when the land was stolen. We have been stripped, robbed and raped of all our natural resources. What the Government calls Crown Land belongs to aboriginal people. I'd love to tell the world how badly we have been treated and your government literally stole this country from my people. I am tired and I want some action on what this Government is going to do to compensate my people. There will forever be first nation's people in this country. I don't ever remember a time when I was young, it didn't matter what we needed to help make our lives a little easier, we always had to go and see the Indian agent and was made to carry a letter of authorization to cut wood on our own land, to fish and to leave our area to visit my grandmother who lived on the same reserve. I don't remember anyone asking us to show them the letter we had to permit us to fish. These are some of the atrocities that first nation's people succumbed to. It all started with not allowing us to be who we are, and we survived.

Dad's Rooster

—➤●◄—

DAD HAD A ROOSTER THAT HE cherished very much and he even gave him a name which escapes me right now. He entered it in the Mohawk Fair and won first prize. He really watched over this bird. Mom would send us three girls to the hen house to get eggs which she would trade for other things and every time we would go to gather eggs this rooster would get very ugly. He chased us and literally flew and sat on our backs, we were all afraid of him. One day as I went to get eggs with the basket on my arm, Barbara and Carmel were watching as I went in the henhouse. The chickens ran out cackling and running in every direction, I guess they scared the rooster. It flew up and lit on Carmel's back. She was crying and swatting trying to get the rooster off her back. Mom came running out of the house to see what was going on and what was causing all the commotion. I guess at this point we were tired of what the rooster had been doing so mom decided to have him for supper.

Dad was away working all day and didn't know what was going on. We must have chased the rooster around the door yard all morning when Barb and I finally caught it. I had it by the legs and I remember being knocked down a few times. Mom told me to lay his head on the chopping block. I did and she chopped off its head. She brought up the axe and closed her eyes and axe fell just below its combs. Mom opened her eyes and looked down at it and decided she hadn't wasted anything. I let go of the rooster by this time and it was still running all over the door yard. I didn't know what was happening. This bird should have just lain down. Finally it came to rest in some prickly rose bushes. We got all scratched up when we finally pulled it out of the bush. Dad came home from helping the farmers with their daily chores and said to mom,

"Supper smells good, what are we having?"

"Your crazy old rooster."

Dad wanted to know "Did he put up a good fight?"

Mom said "Oh yes, the girls chased him around the door yard all morning."

Dad said "We shouldn't eat him, he's old and he's going to be tough as leather."

Mom said "Maybe not, I boiled it for four hours. Well, are you going to have your night time meal or not?"

By this time dad was getting over his initial shock and he had his supper but he only ate the dumplings. Dad said they were the best dumplings he had ever eaten. Periodically dad would chop off the heads of a chicken or two but this only happened when we had nothing in our trap lines. A few days later someone was talking to dad and told him they were late getting out of bed that morning.

"Were you sick?" he said.

"No, I was listening for your rooster and he never crowed."

Dad said "He will never crow again."

The other person asked "Why?"

"Kathleen and the girls chopped off his head yesterday and we had him for our night time meal."

Dad left the neighbours and came home. It was rather sad listening to dad talk about his prize winning rooster. I didn't laugh but everyone else did. My heart went out to my dad and he never did get another rooster.

A Wedding At Chic's House

SOMETIME IN THE MID NINETEEN THIRTIES there was a special gathering at Chic's house when she lived in Point Anne. I was just big enough to stand on my tip toes and hold my hands at the edge of the table and peak at some of the dishes that were there. The table was set and it was beautiful. I heard someone whisper and touch me on the shoulder and I put my hands behind my back. My, what a lovely sight it was, the table had flowers on it and there were really nice chairs that I had not seen before but it seems they were borrowed from the Orange Lodge and ribbons and bows tied all over the house. Mom and her sisters were busy along with Chic to make sure everything was perfect and ready for whatever was supposed to happen; I found out later that it was a wedding for one of mom's sisters. Everyone was in a very happy mood. I remember being outdoors with some of my cousins but wasn't allowed off the front stoop to run around on the ground and get dirty. I had on a little yellow dress Chic had made me and the reason I remember it was because mom put it in a big oval picture frame along with a lock of papadad's hair. I recall seeing it hanging on the wall in the parlor when I was growing up. She even smocked the bodice part to make it look like a dolls dress, I wasn't very big.

The house was a buzz of activity that day with people going and coming and visiting with each other. In the meantime dad had asked me to go with him to the bay where there were a lot of row boats filled with people and some standing on shore; these people had come from Tyendinaga. Dad was helping the women to get out of the boats, some he carried and some he couldn't because they were too heavy. They took off their shoes and walked through the water holding up their dresses. Dad told me to take them to Chic's house since they didn't know where she lived; so here we went with me barefoot leading all these people up the side of the road to Chic's house. I recall doing this quite clearly. Chic's front yard was full of cars, there were people everywhere, most I knew and some I didn't.

It was a sit down meal, I don't know what was being served but it must have been good because the people stayed for a long time. Mom fixed us a dish and we had to sit on the cement stoop to eat our supper and of course we were just giggling. We weren't allowed to take the good dishes outdoors they were afraid we would break them so we ate off tin plates. It was a night time party, I just barely remember everyone clearing the table, washing dishes and putting every thing away. The dining furniture was being moved out in the kitchen to make room for the people to have some fun. There were some men sitting on the stairs playing their musical instruments; all the children were taken upstairs and put to bed and even some of them were on the floor. I remember going to sleep then I would wake up and hear laughter; I sneaked down a few stairs then I could see them dancing and having a whale of a time. Some of the children got up next morning and went downstairs to find some adults in the kitchen but I'm thinking they hadn't gone to bed yet. It took everyone a few days to help Chic clean up the house. When I went down stairs some of the people were eating and some were just standing talking to each other; no one seemed to be in a hurry to go home. Sometime after supper there was another dance and everyone was kicking up their heals having a wonderful time. Some of the people who had gone home earlier returned to join in the festivities.

A Mohawk Fair Gathering

WE WERE HAVING A VERY WARM spring about nineteen thirty seven, I didn't know what time of year it was but Chic told me it was spring. The birds are all back singing and making nests and of course the oopops pond was alive with all sorts of life.

I recall asking papadad "What is all the noise?"

He said "Listen carefully." And I did.

Then I asked him, "What are all the different sounds I hear?"

He said "That's all the frogs and toads having a square dance at the oopops pond and all the rest of the animals are joining in the chorus."

"Can I sing too?"

Papadad said "Yes, go ahead."

I put my hands to my mouth and shouted in the direction of the pond "Go 'round, go 'round."

They all clapped and had loving smiles on their faces, I guess they approved of what I did and I was being a silly little girl who was just full of life.

Our mom and grandmothers had worked hard all winter and spring to get things ready for the Mohawk Fair which takes place in early fall; it was a very important time in our lives. We girls didn't know but the day of the fair had arrived. Mom and our grandmothers had dressed us up in pretty dresses they had made from dyed sugar bags and mine was red, can't remember my sisters dress colours. When I put my dress on I just stood there looking at mom.

She said "Do you like your new dress?"

I said "Oh yes!"

And I hugged her so hard and told her how much I loved her. We looked at each other and she had tears in her eyes but I didn't know why. My dress was a full skirt with a small top and big puffy short sleeves with a red ribbon tied around my waist with a big bow.

Mom said "You can go and wait outside with dad."

I recall her telling dad "Don't let her get dirty."

Dad said "Okay."

When dad saw me he made a big bow and aimed his both arms at me and told me I looked like a little princess. I didn't know what to say so I said nothing. While we were there standing and waiting for my sisters and everyone else to get dressed I was stiff-legged not moving an inch. Finally everyone came out of the house and dad looked at everyone and brushed a tear from his eye and said,

"Is this my family?"

After this emotional minute or two had passed, dad walked over and put our big protective stick across the door which was the symbol that everyone used when no one was home. We all looked beautiful, even papadad was all dressed up and I remember he was happy because he was whistling, something I was supposed to learn.

We all started walking up the beach road towards Shannonville and we looked around as other people were joining us when we came near their homes. I was walking very carefully on the side of the gravel road as not to get dirty and I had my sister Barbara by the hand.

The elders were talking about how important this gathering was and I'm sure there weren't any people left on the beach road when one of them asked,

"Does anyone have a note from the Indian agent?"

They all stopped for a moment then decided they weren't going to worry about it then resumed walking toward Shannonville. Before we arrived at the fair grounds, papadad and my two grandmothers had to have a rest. They sat in the ditch along the York Road just past where the Post Office used to be. Mom gave them each a rag that she had wet with water and vinegar to quench their thirst. Papadad just lay back in the long grass with his knees bent and gave a long sigh while he rested. I remember because mom brought some fry bread to have for lunch and we hadn't eaten yet so this was a good time to eat. Eventually we started to walk again, this was some time after lunch and we finally arrived at the fair.

What a joyous sight it was. Before we entered the fair grounds a certain ceremony was to take place. We saw all our cousins, aunties, uncles and other relations. We gathered in three big circles holding on hands and thanked Creator for looking after us while we were walking. We also asked Him to join us at this special time and for being with us on our journey to the Mohawk Fair. Papadad put corn meal around the gate and dad gave us all a piece of cedar, dried grass and a small amount of tobacco and he told us to take it to the main fire pit. There were a lot of people gathered there. One of the people who were there walked around the inner circle with the sweet grass so we could smudge ourselves before entering the fair grounds. He seemed quite surprised that I knew what to do.

He asked me "Who showed you how to do this?"

I told him "My dad and papadad."

He asked me "Do you know why you are doing this?"

I said "To purify my body and to always have good thoughts and a good mind."

We should always have these ceremonies because they were important then as they are now and to keep them always in our mind. After this special time we walked around and visited with a lot of people, some I knew and some I didn't.

A person asked me "Are you going to dance, Margaret?"

I said "Yes, when my dad and papadad start playing their fiddles. I'm always ready to dance."

There were pony rides, horse pulls, stone games the men would play, ball throwing contests, ball kicking contests, racing, games of tag everyone played and we even had a ballgame with a little ball and a little stick. Some would hit the ball and if they couldn't run someone else had to run for them and everyone got so mixed up and laughing so hard they all had to quit playing for a minute and sit on the ground to gather their strength. Finally it would resume and we played most of the afternoon. We all had a wonderful time and a great visit with all our people.

I heard fiddle music in the distance and told mom,

"Dad was playing now."

She said "Okay, you go join dad and papadad and I'll see you in a minute."

I was really pleased to see my papadad playing there; I kissed him and said, "I'm here."

He said "Okay Dolly, are you ready?"

I said "Let's go."

The first tune he played was 'Little Burnt Potato' and boy did I dance. Papadad hollered "I'm tired."

I danced a lot that day and there were a lot of people playing different instruments. This is a little insight into how we spent some of our time just having fun. As I remember and look back at these special gatherings, they were essential for our people, this is why we really have to bring all these things forward. It is who we are. Let's not let anyone take any of this away from us anymore. Hang on to it; it belongs to you and me.

A House On The Hill

MY GRANDMOTHER CHIC ONCE LIVED ON the hill before you get to the bridge over the river where the police station now stands. That is also the same place where the school I attended was when I first started and Leslie Claus was my teacher. As far as I can remember there was one large room full of kids and we were all the same size. I remember very clearly there was no English spoken there because we were trying to preserve our culture. Anyway she had a small garden that mom and dad made for her where she grew her own vegetables and there was rhubarb all around the garden. There was also a large apple tree in the front yard and towards the house there was a plum tree. I remember going there and she showed me how to pick the weeds from the garden. She had quite a large patch of potatoes she and I put in, every potato I put in the ground she would say "Eyes up!" We would have a little laugh and I said "Just like papadad says." She just nodded. I stayed with her for a while and helped her tend the garden. When the potatoes got a little bigger her and I would pick some rhubarb leaves and I would help carry them into the house where she would cook them in a big pot. When the pot cooled enough she would strain the juice through a cloth, we put it in a pail and carried it out to the garden and poured it on the potatoes using an old dipper.

"Why are you doing this?" I asked.

She told me "It was to keep the bugs from eating the potatoes."

Chic was really clever I thought to get rid of the bugs in this manner. We had quite a discussion about the bugs and rhubarb juice.

She said "When you get older you will learn all about what is a good bug and what is a bad bug."

So over my growing years I never harmed anything. That was the best thing I could do and I wouldn't get in trouble.

I remember we had a lot of fun when we were visiting Chic. Once when we were down there dad fixed a broken floor board. He got a board from the barn. This barn was always full of hay and we kids would always be playing in the hay loft. Dad finished the floor boards and him and Uncle Ike, my grandmother's brother, had to put some beams under the floor to make it more stable. It took quite a while to do this. After they finished the floor they banked up the outside of the house and fixed the outside of the windows for winter.

Ferg McFarland owned a grocery store in Shannonville and he was also the undertaker. He had asked mom if grandma could use some wall paper. He said they were just ends of some rolls and all different patterns. Grandma said that she didn't care because it would be clean. My aunts Mabel, Winnie and Phoebe and mom started preparing the walls for papering. Chic made some stuff in a big tub that was sitting on the floor, I didn't know what it was but she was stirring and stirring and it seemed things were not going well for her.

I looked at it "What is it?" I asked.

Chic said "What do think it is?"

"It looks like chicken and dough gods that mom used to make."

That is what everyone called dumplings. Chic sat down on the floor and picked me up and she was giggling really hard, so was I.

Mom asked "What's the matter?"

Chic said "Dolly thinks it looks like chicken and dough gods".

Everyone stopped working and sat on their chairs and we all laughed so hard we were crying and grandma couldn't get her breath. We sat there for a long time and finally Chic scrambled to her feet,

"This calls for a cup of tea".

Chic made some green tea and gave us all some. We had to wait while she had a smoke on her pipe for a little while then they all went back to work again. It took a long time to get all the walls prepared for the paper; they didn't get it done in one day.

The next day they started to put up the wall paper and everyone was helping. Chic didn't get all the lumps out of the paste and after a few rows of paper were up I saw the lumps and I would put my fingers on them and they would slither away and join the other lumps. I remember using the rolling pin to try to flatten them; I was just trying to help. They must have worked for days it seemed. They finally got it all done and while everyone was still there and they cleaned the house. Some time after our night time meal, people began to show up. They all had food which they placed on the table in the front room. I don't remember what the occasion was; maybe it was a house warming. We never seemed to need a reason. I don't remember who all came but I do remember Johnny Sero's mother. She brought her banjo and boy could she ever play. It wasn't long before the house filled with people.

Dad said "It was a good thing that Ike and I fixed the floor boards."

Johnny Sero's mother said "Have you got your fiddle, Budge?"

Dad said "I never go anywhere without it."

Uncle Ike spoke up "I'll get my mouth organ."

When uncle Ike was playing his mouth organ sitting beside dad, once in a while his eyes would rove over to the lumps in the paper. Dad asked him,

"What are you looking at?"

"All these lumps in the paper." he said.

"Those aren't lumps; they're all the people who died in this house trying to get in from the other side of the wall."

Uncle Ike said,"Oh, shut up and just play your fiddle."

There were people everywhere. Mom stood on a chair and gave a yip and dad and everyone else started to play their musical instruments. Mom got off her chair sat it over beside dad and they had a good old square dance. Mom called for the dance in Mohawk. She did this all the time and everyone seemed to know what to do. A good time was had by all. As I said I wasn't sure what the reason was except everyone was all together again. We never needed a reason to gather at someone's house, it just happened. This was happening all the time. These are some of my memories of when I was small living at Tyendinaga. As I grew older I always thought this is what everyone did because that's what happened when we all got together. We were all related whether we actually were or not and that's what made all these gatherings so very special. We all knew each other very well and I felt the people were very strong as far as their beliefs and laws were concerned. This is the reason why I will always remember these special gatherings because the elders used this time for teaching and what a teaching job they did. We have to get back to these teachings; it really is part of us. I will always be indebted to all my people.

A Visitor Came

=>●<=

It happened to be sometime in the winter, there was a lot of snow on the ground. My mom and dad and two sisters and I were getting a ride to Shannonville with Uncle Oliver Hill who had two horses and a big sleigh. I can't remember why we were going but had to have been for something special. It turned out we went for groceries for all the people who lived there. There were quite a few older people who couldn't get to the village that's why we went. When we got to Shannonville and the groceries were loaded and we were heading back home it started to snow by the time we left the village. Our sleigh was piled up with all sorts of food. I recall we three girls were sitting on top of some of the boxes and hanging on for dear life. It was taking us longer to get home, it was getting darker and it was snowing really hard by this time.

We got all the way back to Beverley Brant's laneway where we would meet her and go to the mission school together, I hated that place but that's another story, the horses got stuck in the snow. We had to get off the sleigh. Mom, dad and Uncle Oliver had to take some of the food off and set it on the side of the road. We waited there with mom until dad came back with our smaller sleigh. Dad put some of the food on this sleigh and headed for home, I'm sure we were there half the night. I remember us three girls lying down in the snow, we probably wanted to go to sleep, and mom and Uncle Oliver were chasing us trying to keep us awake. Dad had returned with the sleigh to take more groceries and this time he brought Joker Brant to help. Dad also brought with him a lantern and he gave it to mom so she could take us home. Dad and Uncle Oliver stayed with the horses and groceries all night. When mom left with us dad kept hollering at her to make sure we were all right.

Mom asked me "Are you okay?"

I said "Yes and I'm glad I got my blue bloomers on."

Mom just looked at me and smiled. Everyone was still busy the next day delivering the groceries. We were in bed early that night. I remember papadad asking mom where she went for groceries. Papadad didn't realize it had snowed so much and didn't know we weren't home all night.

The next morning when we woke papadad's boots were facing in opposite directions. Mom said "A visitor came last night."

I looked around and didn't see anyone different.

"Look what they left you girls on the chair, three oranges."

I didn't know what they were; I thought it was a ball.

Mom said "No, no, you don't play with it, you eat it."

That was the first time in my life that I had ever seen an orange. Mom peeled it and gave it to us. I didn't like it very much so I kept the orange in my coat pocket until it was very hard. A few days later I went to the barn and gave it to our horse Molly. She turned her head and looked at me with funny eyes that were big and oogley, the funniest look I'd ever seen. She coughed a few times and that's the last that I saw the orange.

Papadad asked me "Did you like your orange?"

I said "I don't know, I gave it to the horse."

"Did she choke?"

"I don't know, she just looked at me funny and coughed a few times and it was gone." Someone had once given us a banana and I didn't like it either. I couldn't seem to swallow it; I told mom they didn't cook it right.

Jakey Brant would sometimes leave candy in a hole in an old post at the corner of our yard; I thought Jakey was the one who gave us the orange. As I grew up and remembered this event I think it may have been Christmas and the visitor who left the orange was supposed to be Santa, but I can honestly say that I never heard either of these words spoken in our house by anyone because we never did celebrate this time of year. We only celebrated the coming of winter, dad called them changes, and we always had special ceremonies. So nothing changed except the oranges turned up.

I grew up at a time when my people always pulled together; we went through some really tough times. We always had each other and a house full of love. They kept a lot of things from the children so as I grew older I knew things were very bad sometimes, but no one ever complained, they just did whatever they had to do to make sure we all survived day by day. They were teaching important lessons every day to make sure we understood and learned these lessons and hoped I supposed we would always remember them in our adult life, I certainly did. Our past is very important to us. We can't go forward until we know where we came from. I have always been a strong believer in our culture and our way of life; I'm hoping most people still feel the same way. It's not only our language; it is our whole way of life that we have to bring back now. I am personally more comfortable knowing where I came from and knowing who I am. This is a good time in my life when I can know the freedom I once had as a child. I have been reintroducing certain elements back into my life that never really went away, like my language, spirituality that has always been there and our great law. All these things have to be there in our everyday lives. It is who we really are.

Visiting Chic

MOM AND DAD AND WE THREE girls walked from the beach through the swamp, part of the bush where we gathered our wood without a permit, to visit my grandmother Chic who lived on Lower Slash Road. Her brother lived with her, his name was Isaiah and we called him uncle Ike.

Chic lived in a big two story wood frame house. It was situated on the North side of the road; I do believe it was the last house on the road. Chic was always glad to see us. We would stay for a few days because dad and uncle Ike had to do some fixing up around the house. I recall them putting a tin roof on part of the kitchen. We brought Chic a rain barrel from home so she could catch some fresh rain to water her garden. There was a creek that ran down that way on the South side of the Slash road but it was too far to carry water because it was down hill going and uphill coming back.

Mom helped Chic do some preserves for winter. She stored them all in the cellar. You had to enter the cellar from the outside of the house and when they didn't have to go down there uncle Ike had a steel rod and the biggest lock I'd ever seen on the door.

Dad used to laugh at him and say "Well, none of the little people are going to get in and neither will the big ones."

It sounded funny even in Mohawk; they both started laughing at the same time.

Uncle said "We are going to have a special supper tonight."

He had bagged three or four rabbits and sis was going to roast them. Along with this Chic cooked some cabbage and other vegetables. After it was cooked and on the table and Creator thanked for the food, I looked and had no idea what it was but we weren't allowed to say we didn't like it. We all ate some, I must admit I really liked it especially the rabbit.

Uncle Ike asked dad "Would it be okay to have a thank you ceremony in the kitchen by the stove?"

Dad said "Yes, it is always okay with Creator to have these ceremonies no matter where you are the only special thing about it is why we are having it."

Dad started off thanking Creator for the food we had for our night time meal. He gave some of it to aunt Jeanette to take home; she just lived up the road from us. I went with dad out in the bush to give thanks to the Creator for the rabbit's spirit and dad hung a small piece of meat in the tree. We had a good meal and all went to bed with full tummies and we were satisfied spiritually. A few stories were told then we girls went to bed upstairs while the older people played cards. They must have been having a lot of fun because there was a lot of laughing going on.

The spiritual part of our lives was dad and papadad's role and they were kept busy because there was always a need for a spiritual dependability. Dad was responsible for our sacred fire. He was taught about all these things by his father and of course he taught me. I learned from papadad until he got sick and went to the spirit world. As I grew older dad took over and he carried on from there teaching me. It was an ongoing event everyday. We always had certain ceremonies when we visited Chic because she was the person responsible for certain things in the ceremonies because she had the Talking Feather.

I recall being down at Chic's after dad and uncle Ike finished fixing up the house and we had all gone down to the river that ran past her house on the South side of the road to go fishing; we caught some pickerel. After we had enough fish we had a ceremony right there on the river bank and Chic had her Eagle Feather and I was shown how to clean fish and most important what to say to thank Creator for the catch. While we were still at the river I noticed one of the fish's eyes was not where it was supposed to be. I was looking and looking at its eye and Chic said "What's wrong?"

I said "I don't know, something is wrong with the fish's eye."

I picked up the fish and held it in my apron and remember trying to fix it. It felt funny when I touched it. Chic was sitting on the ground and I sat down beside her. I touched its eye again and it really had a strange feeling to me. I pinched my thumb and index finger together and rubbed my finger on Chic's dress and was making all sorts of noises and looked at Chic with a little screwed up face. She told me I had umpteen wrinkles in my brow head; she was talking a foreign language. I didn't know what she meant. She let me hold the Eagle Feather and I remember asking the Creator to help the fish find its way home. Chic told me to put the eye back in the river. I did what was asked of me. It took a long time for me to really forget about the special fish that only had one eye.

The next morning came and we all got up before Grandfather Sun. Dad and uncle Ike had to build an extension on a ladder they had in order to be able to put a new roof on part of the kitchen. I remember going up the road and asking aunt Jeanette, Chic's friend, for some old nails she said they could have. She gave me some in a bag. I took them home in a round about way. By this time they had finished the ladder so they were going to start putting the roof on the kitchen. After they got that finished they both went to see what they could do to prepare the barn that was in need of repairs. Other people used to store hay in the barn; that's where we would put our horse when visiting Chic and uncle Ike in the winter. We always had a good time at Chic's and it was good for mom too because mom was very close to her mother. It was nice to have visited all these places and for me to be able to remember where all these meetings took place.

A lot of people came when we had our night time ceremony. After the ceremony was over everyone sat around the fire in a big circle and visited with each other. I'm sure if I happened to walk through the field now I would be able to find the very spot where we were fishing. The fish was fried in butter after being rolled in flour and pepper. Of all the fish I've eaten, pickerel by far is my favorite; it even tastes better when cooked outside. We really did have a lot of wonderful times together when I was growing up and we had some not so very nice times also but we all got through it together. I thank all the people who were there for their love and understanding and for teaching me all the things that are so important. This is one of the reasons that we have to bring all these sacred things forward and never leave them behind. Think about how important all these things were to us so many years ago and all the hardship and secretive times our people went through to keep our ways alive and I know in my heart that they didn't want us to leave them all behind. We fought hard to preserve our ways so bring them all forward and embrace them.

Celebrating Our Togetherness

ONE HOT SUMMER DAY ABOUT NINETEEN thirty-seven we all went down to the beach. The children were playing in the water of course and the adults were sitting around on the sand talking about whatever. Dad and my two uncles were out on the bay fishing and managed to get a lot of fish that day, and whoever showed up for supper stayed because we all had plenty. Mom and some of the women got up from where they were sitting and mom took a big frying pan down from the tree that dad had hung there for everyone to use. The rest of the women were busy making fry bread. I remember a piece of the bread dough had fallen in the fire on some red -hot coals.

One of the women said, "I found a new way to cook our bread."

They all just laughed and said, "Oh Oh."

Mom said, "Let me know how you intend to pick the coals from it."

Everyone laughed and she said, "I haven't figured that out yet."

I think it was Mrs. Con Maracle who said, "I'll take it home and use it for a door stop."

I asked "What is a door stop?"

They just snickered and so did I. It seems to me that we were laughing all the time. We all had a wonderful supper and I can remember some of the people who were there; Johnny and Joe Sero, my two uncles Jim and Nick Sero, Chic and Rose my two grammas, my papadad, Jakey Brant, Joker Brant and his family and all the people who lived around us. We each had a tin plate that we ate off of; after we finished eating we washed our plates in the sand, rinsed it off in the water and laid them all in the long grass to dry.

We all decided to go for a swim and as I said before it was really hot and none of us had a swimsuit. They all left their cloths on except for the children who only wore their underwear. I had those blue bloomers on and every time I would squat down in the water and stand up again the legs would fill with water and down I would go. I could hardly stand up or hold my pants up, and everyone was just roaring they were laughing so hard. I guess I was just being silly. My parents couldn't swim either so they and most everyone else were sitting down in the water. The women were all sitting in circles cackling like chickens and having a grand old time when all of a sudden Mom gave a big war hoop and everyone just froze, they all looked like statues. This only lasted a couple of seconds. Mom moved so quickly, that was the first time in my life I ever saw my mom jump. She called for dad who came running in the deep water to see what was wrong. I just stood there wondering what was happening and mom asked dad to see what had bit her when she was sitting in the water. Dad looked and saw a little crab. After this episode with the crab mom would only go in the water up to her knees. We all laughed at her so hard we were all rolling around in the water because mom was so big and this little crab had chased her out of the water.

When all this excitement was over things calmed down

somewhat and Johnny Sero thought he would try his hand at swimming. So when he dove down in the water his swim trunks fell down and mom screamed,

"Black snake, Johnny!"

Of course I didn't know what this meant. I got out of the water because I thought mom saw a snake. After that event everyone called him 'Black snake Johnny'. We always seemed to be able to have an exciting and memorable time when we were all together.

A true story of what happened at Tyendinaga Mohawk Beach when I was a little girl. I loved being there.

We had a lot of special gatherings and every time we did something new happened. So I experienced new things everyday. Johnny was never able to live down his special name that was given to him. When I think about these times I can still remember them being silly times. They are the people who made me who I am. We should be able to do some of these things now. It was very important for people to get together in the thirties and forties; I know they saw each other every day just to check in to see how each other was. There was always a great effort put forward by the younger people, I'm referring to my parents age, to make sure the older people were always attended to in the most caring and loving way. These are some of the things I remember as a child. I've carried these feelings throughout my life and it's been good.

Uncle Marshall And His Leeks

An introduction to Marshall Lewis. He was my father's first cousin who lived at Tyendinaga on the Beach Road; uncle Marshall had a farm where he grew corn and other vegetables and big fields of tomatoes for the canning factory in Shannonville where my mom and dad worked. My sister Barbara and I would walk about a mile in our bare feet to pick some wild leeks that were growing in the corner of the corn field. We didn't know what these things were except they smelled like onions; anyway mom would cook them with potatoes and make soup, it was really good.

We were coming past there another time before the corn was picked and Barb and I crawled through a hole in the fence. All of a sudden we heard a loud noise; we both looked up and saw this awful looking black thing coming through the corn patch towards us. We both began to scream because we were scared thinking that one of the scare crows had come alive. Barb and I were hanging on to each other for dear life and crawled towards the fence. I tried to push her through the hole in the fence and she got stuck and was unable to free herself. It turned out it was uncle Marshall scaring us. We were so scared we couldn't move.

He asked us," What are you doing?"

We told him, "We came to get some wild leeks that were growing at the edge of his corn field so mom could make some soup."

"Okay" he said," I was only playing with you."

It was quite a long time before Barb and I went picking leeks again.

I remember those times like it was yesterday. We had a lot of places to visit; it was grandmas, grandpas, aunts, uncles or cousins. Some of the people were related and some were not but we called them all the same out of respect as children and I have always remembered. A wonderful life.

A Gathering For Chic

SOMETIME AROUND NINETEEN THIRTY SIX THERE was a gathering
of my family that took place in an area called Ferry Lane on the
territory. I can't remember what it was all about but I do recall it
was important because people did this only on special occasions.
We had gathered over the weekend at a location where my auntie
Mabel and uncle Albert Culbertson lived with their family. She
was my mom's sister. Mom and all her sisters were busy trying
so hard to get things in order while the children were outside
playing.

Picture in your mind the comic strip Li'l Abner. What I
remember of this comic is only the pictures because I couldn't
read yet. Anyway, the biffy was parked on a little hill with a lot
of rocks around it and a fare ways from the house. Someone had
put a black stovepipe out through the roof which was crooked,
even the door wouldn't shut properly. Betty, my cousin and I
took hold of each other by the hand and hopped all the way
along this narrow path that led to our destination. On our way
we decided we had better hurry up so we ran the rest of the way.
Once inside, the seat was built up too high for little people. I
helped Betty get on the seat and she had lowered her clothes to

her ankles then I had to brace my heels against the boards the seats were built on so I could sit down. I just got sitting when Betty let a terrifying scream.

I asked her "What's wrong?" in the same kind of scream.

She said "Something's bit my fanny!"

I jumped down and asked her "Can you move?"

She said "No."

So I ran down the path pulling up my clothes as I went back to the house to get someone to come and see what happened to Betty. Everyone came running thinking she had fallen in and me screaming,

"No! no! She didn't." But no one was listening to me.

I'm sure by now the few neighbours who lived along the same road were wondering why everyone was running up the hill to the biffy. Mom and aunt Mabel and aunt Winnie were trying so hard to run up the hill 'cause they were three little fat people and were stumbling and waving their arms in the air and hollering; it was quite a sight. When they reached Betty she was still sitting there crying, someone picked her up and took her outside, laid her on the ground to see what had happened. Nobody did anything until Chic got there and she was the last one to reach the biffy while Betty was laying there with her clothes around her knees. Chic looked to see what the matter was and told Betty she will be okay,

"It was a bumble bee that stung you; we'll put some medicine on it when we get back to the house."

Betty didn't even answer. She wasn't too active the rest of the day; she just sat on a day bed with a pillow under her fanny.

After that dangerous episode had passed, we all went down to the bay and had a wash and everyone who was supposed to be there had arrived except for uncle Albert, he was the last one to come home. It seems we waited for him forever. I remember everyone called him 'crow'. I didn't know why, they had nick names for everyone and this was his. Just before he arrived I ran into the house and announced

"I saw crow."

And Chic said "Is he walking down the road Dolly?"

I said "No, he's flying."

Everyone sat down wherever they were and had a good old fashioned laugh. I laughed too but didn't know why. Everyone seemed to be having a good time except for Betty. Uncle Albert finally came home, it must have been around our supper time meal and everyone was glad to see him.

At this time Chic thanked Creator again for our health, for being together and for the food we had received from Mother Earth, but before we were allowed to eat, all the grandchildren who were old enough served food to all the elders first; it was always that way. We had a lot of food. After we had eaten we put our tin plates in the wagon and took them down to the bay to wash them. When we arrived back at the house mom and her sisters and brothers had announced that they had a big surprise for their mother. Chic had to close her eyes and sit in the middle of the floor on a chair while we all joined hands and made a big circle around her. Then mom came through the door with this humungous cake that had fire all over it. I thought what is this; I've never seen this before. I'll never forget the look on everyone's face. Mom asked Chic to open her eyes which she did and then put her hands to her face and started to cry. Then someone started to sing happy birthday. I just listened because I didn't really understand what was happening, any way I didn't know the words. Mom put this big cake on the table and it had something written on it and I asked mom what it was.

She said "It says 'Happy Birthday Mother from your children and also Happy Birthday Chic from all the little ones'.

I should have known it was to be something special because

dad and uncle Ike had a fire going all day. I wandered over to visit dad at the fire and we talked for a while.

He asked me "Do you want to know what's going on?"

I said "Yes."

Dad asked me "Would you remember if I told you?"

I said "Uh huh."

Then he smiled at me in the most fatherly and lovingly way and said "I know you will remember. This is an honouring ceremony for your grandmother."

I said "You mean Chic."

Dad said "Yes."

During the festivities dad got out his fiddle and uncle Ike got his mouth organ and as soon as everyone else had heard the news of the special birthday honouring Chic it wasn't long before other people began to arrive. I do remember this event and everyone had a wonderful time and Chic was happy too. They had a square dance in the door yard and mom called for the dance in Mohawk. Everyone who was dancing was getting their skirts and feet tangled up in the long grass. It turned out most of the time the people were just hopping around. I don't know how long it went on but when we all woke up in the morning everyone was still there. As the children went to sleep they were all carried to one big room and were laid down on some straw ticks to sleep.

This was an important gathering for Chic so she could celebrate her fifty sixth birthday with her whole family and all the rest of the people who knew her. We should honour all our elders more often and let them know that they are very important to us all, I always have. I had wonderful times when I was with Chic. She was always very important to me.

Sometimes when I get lonesome for her I just close my eyes and be very quiet and she comes to me in my thoughts, and I remember the things we talked about and what she taught me and she told me to never change and be very proud of who you are. I remember these soft spoken words Chic said. She was always there when I got in trouble and she comforted me.

The Importance Of Being Together

I can't remember if it was winter or not, there didn't seem to be much snow but there was an important gathering at the beach. The pools of water that were lying in the fields were all frozen. These pools were in the hay fields and of course there was hay stubble sticking up through the ice.

One-day mom's sister, aunt Winnie and uncle Jimmie and all the kids came to visit. We were all glad to see each other and we hugged. They bundled us all up and we were allowed to go outside to play and we headed for the hay field; I'm sure Doug was the only one who had skates so we all started running all over the field chasing each other in every direction. We played tag and all sorts of other games. Now Doug remembered he was supposed to let us have a turn on his skates, he was a bit bigger and so were his feet. We didn't all take turns because there was too many of us and it was getting late in the day. I do recall us being able to go back outside after supper and Doug being the oldest, was responsible for carrying dad's lantern and the moon was quite bright that night. It came my turn to learn how to skate and I was certain I didn't want to try because I had such a hard time learning to walk in my new snow shoes so I decided to sit on the skates. He had tied the laces together, this is how he pulled us all around the ice. The younger children were just lying down on the ground. I know we were all quite tired.

Mom was close with her siblings and it was special that they had a chance to visit with each other. Everyone must have stayed all night because they were all there in the morning when I got up. We had something to eat. Chic peeled and sliced some potatoes and cooked them right on top of the stove, my were they ever good, and seeing there were so many people she even stuck some potatoes on the side of the stove to cook. We had these kinds of potatoes quite often. We also had toasted frybread that was done in the same manner. Uncle Jimmie and dad took our big sleigh and cut down some wood, enough to last for a while. I found out later about woodcutting that we had to have permission to cut our own wood. Some people had cut wood without permission and they were missing for a while, I believe they were in jail. They had cut enough wood for uncle Jimmie to take home and they asked uncle Oliver if he would deliver the wood to uncle Jimmie's house. He said he would use the team of horses and sleigh to take the wood and them all home when they were ready to go. They lived somewhere around what is now known as Ridge Road East of Norway's Road on a farm.

Mom and aunt Winnie made some bread. Mom had no bread pans so she braided the bread and laid them on a large piece of tin that dad had pounded in the shape of a square. They cooked a lot of things that day; so when they left to go home they took half of everything with them. We watched them and walked with them for a while. Aunt Winnie waved and blew some kisses and told us not to cry, she would see us soon and we better go home now. I remember walking backwards for a long time and they became smaller and smaller and I got lonesome all over again. We did see each other quite often and we always were happy to see each other. We were more like brothers and sisters than like cousins. This is the way things are supposed to be. I've been told by non-natives that you can't keep bringing your past with you. I wouldn't be able to go on not knowing what I know, I certainly wasn't raised that way. Our past is very important to us. The mere thought of our past does have a powerful impact on our lives and our future generations. We are different from non-natives. We do have to remember our past.

Mr. Bullfrog

———➤●◄———

ONE DAY WHEN MR. BULLFROG WAS swimming around the neighbourhood pond when across the pond sitting on a big green lily pad was the most beautiful frog he had ever seen. He thought to himself,

"I think I'll swim over and acquaint myself to her."

As he swam closer he was wondering what to say. He peeked at her and with his nose just below the water and all she could see was his big bulging eyes. She covered her mouth with her front foot and began to laugh silently. She was very careful not to upset him. He smiled at her and put his front foot on the edge of the lily pad and asked permission to climb aboard. She thought for a moment then said okay. They sat there for a while not saying a word then she noticed that he didn't look like she did.

"How come you're not green?" she asked.

"Oh, I'm a bullfrog, that's why my colour is brown and I have lumps on my skin."

"What is your name?" she asked.

"Sam." He answered. "And what is your name?"

"Ella."

"Oh, what a pretty name, can I come and visit you again

sometime?"

"Yes." She said.

After they dated for a while he asked her to marry him.

"You'll have to ask my father, he's the biggest green frog in the kingdom." She said.

He finally got up enough courage to visit her dad and asked him if he could marry his daughter. They talked for a long time and nothing was settled at that visit, so they had several more meetings to attend. Older frog didn't know what to say. He talked to his daughter first and tried to explain to her why she shouldn't marry Sam, not because he's brown and has lumps on his skin but because he wasn't an ordinary green frog.

"I understand, dad, but I do love him and he loves me and I don't understand what all the fuss is about.

"Have you thought about where you and Sam are going to live?"

Ella told her father "Sam and I have strong legs and can hop to another nearby pond."

Dad said "Okay, but if you can't find any room to live there you and Sam can always hop back here and find a good place to live in the Northwest corner of the pond; there you and Sam will find plenty of room to make a nice home and there's a lot of big lily pads there for you two to use and just sit and sun yourselves."

So off Sam and Ella went in search of a home before they were married. They finally returned to visit her parents and set the date for two weeks later.

The big day had arrived; Sam and Ella were married sitting on the big green lily pad where he first met her. It was a grand affair, everyone who lived in the pond turned out for the big event. The frogs on both sides of the family decided to have a dance; they all began by hopping around to the croaking and singing all night long. Sam and Ella were very happy; they returned to their corner of the pond and made sure they didn't wake their neighbours who were ducks and geese. Everyone was happy for them and they lived there for ever as Mr. and Mrs. Sam Bullfrog.

Mother Groundhog

—━►●◄━—

THIS STORY WAS TOLD TO ME by my Papadad. A long time ago a mother Groundhog had little ones and she hid them in a hollow log which became their home. Mother would leave them for long stretches at a time. One day in early spring not long after they were born some of her babies wandered out of the log and couldn't believe their eyes; they were so amazed at what they saw. They put their little paws up to their mouths and were silenced because of the wonder and beauty they had seen. Now they knew where their mother had been going all this time so they turned and ran back down into the log to tell their brothers and sisters of all the wonders outside and urged them to come out. The sun was shining and it was warm and to their amazement along came a mother raccoon and her babies. They sniffed each other then everyone toddled away. After the little raccoons were gone they wondered who they were. Now with all the things that they had tasted such as the new tender grasses and shoots they had a great feast and a belly ache to boot. Mother came home to find that her babies had all disappeared and she became quite upset. The baby groundhogs were running around playing but had traveled a little too far from their log and mom had a reason to be concerned. She stood up on her hind legs, looked and called to them to come home in a high squeaky voice but they were having too much fun. Her voice would change when she was scolding her babies and she began to panic. Papadad said he squatted down and whispered to her what was wrong then they both became very silent and she just kept making squeaky sounds but not very loud. Still squatting he tried to mimic her but she just stared at him. Then he whispered to her in a calm manner that he was offering to help her find her babies; this is what he thought was wrong with her. She didn't do any thing to show that she was afraid and he didn't understand. He took off in the bush in one direction very quietly; she followed him so he told her in Mohawk to go look in another direction. She must have understood because she changed direction. Everything turned out for the best. We found her babies safe and sound, all jumping and running around playing. She didn't seem to be too angry at first but she scolded them in a loving way and he imagined she asked them to never do that again. They had a lot of important lessons to learn before they could be on their own. They all seemed to obey and I'm sure lived to have babies of their own because we still see them today. She wanted only to keep them safe so she scolded them with her little squeaks and chatters and they listened to their mom and learned a lesson in life called just how to be careful.

The Bald Eagle

A LONGTIME AGO IN NATIVE STORIES, they were trying to find a bird that could fly to the Sky World where the Creator lived; this bird had to be powerful and strong. The people were all standing in a sacred circle when all of a sudden a crow dropped by so they had a conversation with him and told him what they were looking for and what his duties would be. The people asked crow,

"Do you understand what we are looking for? You should be strong, wise and powerful."

Crow said, "I understand." Before he flew away from the people he preened himself for the long flight. As he flew away the people watched him for a long time but he didn't seem to be heading upwards. He wasn't gone very long when the people held a council and decided he wasn't the right bird; so when crow came back he told them he wasn't able to fly high enough and the people thanked him for his honesty. Crows feelings weren't hurt, he just wanted to be a crow and live and be able to tease other birds and animals.

The word got around in the bird world and before long Mr. Raven came by to offer his services so again the people told him what they were looking for in this special bird. He flew away and his mind wasn't on what he was supposed to do either. He saw a flock of ravens and all he wanted was go and visit and he forgot what he was asked to do. Raven didn't even bother to explain to the people what really happened in stead he flew down among his friends to have some fun. One of his friends asked him,

"What did the two leggeds want with you?"

He told them what they wanted and he said, "I just don't want to do that sort of thing with my life, I have more important things to do."

"Like what?" said one of his friends.

"Oh, let me see, just tease the people, I know they don't like my beautiful voice."

"You've got to be kidding." Said another friend.

Finally along came a most impressive bird from the bird world. He was again given the same request so he flew away and he was gone for days. He flew so high that when he looked back down to earth it became quite small. He thought to himself 'what am I doing'. After he was soaring for a while on some nice warm updrafts he rather enjoyed it and hadn't realized how long he had been gone or how far he had traveled. He thought he had better get back down to see the people because they might be worried. As he flew back down to Mother Earth it was then he realized just how beautiful everything was and when he returned to the people he was a different looking bird. His head and tail were white from the sun and his eyes were yellow. When he was descending he had discovered something new, he spread his wings forward and spread his tail quite wide to slow himself down. When he finally lit where the people were gathered they were surprised that he hadn't forgotten about them. They told him that he looked a little different from before he left. He told them that he flew so high he nearly reached Grandfather Sun.

That is why today we have the bald eagle because he flew too close to Grandfather Sun and his head and tail were singed. He also has a very loud scream. The people were very happy now; they have a bird who takes their prayers to the Creator. He also warns the people of any danger when he is flying and cries very loud. Our Sacred Bird.

The Oopops Pond

THIS STORY WAS TOLD TO ME by my papadad Lewis when I was a little girl. It seems there was this oopops pond that belonged to Mr. Beaver, his wife and family. It was a small pond. Aboriginal people visited it quite often. One day they were talking to Mr. Beaver to see if he would be willing to share the water.

Mr. Beaver asked, "Why do you want the water?"

The elder said, "Because we have no water to cook with and we are supposed to be learning to share."

Mr. Beaver said," Can I talk this over with my wife?"

The elder said, "Of course."

A few weeks had passed and the elder was sitting at the edge of the pond with his feet dangling in the water when Mr. Beaver spotted him. He swam over to where the elder was sitting.

Mr. Beaver said," How are things going in your world?"

Elder said, "Fine, but my people are getting quite thirsty; have you come to any decision about what we were talking about?"

Mr. Beaver said," Yes, we've decided to let you have some water but what do we get in return?"

Elder said, "We will always plant trees around the pond so

you and your family will always have some food and you will be able to keep your dam in good condition. We will protect you and we won't let anyone harm you since you are very important to us."

Everyone agreed to the decisions that they had talked about.

As time went by the oopops pond grew in size with beautiful big trees and a little waterfall that Mr. Beaver had made so the water could be shared by all. Who shared the oopops pond? It became very important to all kinds of wild life such as small cattails that kept the oopops clean, the birds that nested there, dragonflies, ducks and fish and the elders used the pond also for food and water. It was quite alive in the spring, the frog choirs, birds chirping, the sounds were magnificent and on an old dead tree a little turtle was sunning.

These ponds were quite important to the environment. We need these small and special places for all kinds of life and for us to enjoy. There are a lot of different size oopops around. Papadad called them oopops because one day when we were walking I looked down and saw all these little things jumping around and I was going to say, "Oh, papa." And he said, "I'll take you to the oopops pond" since he knew I was afraid of frogs.

Wren's Song

ONE DAY WREN AND ALL THE other birds went down to the river to get a drink. Just before they got there they all stopped at Moose Creek to eat. This was the dividing line between the territory of themselves and other birds. It was considered Big Foot's favourite fishing hole. Blue Jay volunteered to cook the acorns while everyone else was eating dried deer meat. One acorn kept bubbling up out of the pot, so every time Blue Jay turned her back, Buzzard, being a curious fellow kept watching the acorn and assumed it was the only one in the pot. He would try to snatch it up and eat it but the soup was too hot for him. This is how Buzzard got his burned and bald head. Soon the acorns were cooked. Blue Jay drained the water off and it ran down the hillside and some of the acorns rolled out. This of course caught the attention of the mice, chipmunk and woodpecker.

"I never knew that Mr. Woodpecker would eat acorns or are you just teasing the other animals and birds, or did they scare you when they all started rolling down the bank after I accidentally dropped the big pot they were being cooked in? Whatever the reason there was plenty to go around." Blue Jay said, "You missed the whole lesson about sharing, you became very greedy and that's no way to behave. You are supposed to be setting an example. Can I count on you the next time to do this?"

Mr. Woodpecker listened intently and promised he would behave in a much better manner. They all began fighting over the acorns. Hawk was really concerned about the fighting so he asked Mrs. Wren to sing him a song.

She said, "My singing was not very good."

Hawk said," Go ahead and give it a try."

So Mrs. Wren began to sing. She was right, her singing was awful; so bad that Mr. Hawk took off and flew so far away that he couldn't hear Mrs. Wren singing anymore. It turns out that Mrs. Wren was a beautiful singer compared to the squeaky voice that Mr. Hawk had but they will always remain friends.

Coyote Takes Water From
The Frog People

————➤●◄————

CREATOR MADE THE FROG PEOPLE GUARDIANS of the water so that others wouldn't take advantage of the water; it was their duty to look after all the other animals, birds and other life in the pond. When anyone wanted water to drink or to cook with, they had to ask the Frog people. Coyote came to them one day and said,

"Hey, Frog people, I have a precious shell to offer as payment for a big drink of your water and I would like to drink for a long time because I'm really thirsty from hunting all day."

The Frog people held a council and after some time they decided to give Coyote a drink of water, "Don't forget to give us the shell you said you would."

"Okay, don't you trust me?"

Coyote gave the Frog people the shell and he began to drink. The water that he was drinking was behind a large beaver dam. This is where Coyote drank and drank. He had been there for a very long time and the Frog people were suspicious. Coyote started looking around in a sneaky manner, he didn't want the

Frog people to see him. They figured he was up to no good. Finally the leaders of the Frog people were very concerned and said, "Hey, Coyote, don't you think you have had enough to drink? You sure are drinking more than your fair share."

In the meantime Coyote said, "Let me have just a little bit more."

The Frog people thought for a while and they said, "Okay."

They couldn't understand how a person or animal could drink so much water. Then Coyote started digging out from under the dam a bit of mud that beaver had placed there. When he finished he stood up and hollered,

"That was a great drink of water, just what I needed."

Then just as Coyote was about to leave from behind the dam he slipped and on his way down he took a big piece of dam with him and of course this caused all the water to rush in a torrent and created rivers, ponds and even lakes. The Frog people were very angry at Coyote. Now they were all afraid of him. They all hollered at him,

"Now look what you have done! You've taken all our water!"

Coyote just stood there and laughed at them and said, "It's not right that only one group of people have all the water that you never intended to share. Now the water is in places where all the people and animals can share in this bounty."

Living here on Mother Earth we have to all share the water and other natural things.

The Frog people told Coyote, "You took our water under false pretences which is not a good way to learn to share with each other."

Coyote gave them a silly glance, laid his head to one side and paid no attention. The Frog people scolded him and said,

"You're a trickster; we are going to tell all our friends what kind of animal you really are."

Jake and Lucy Mouse

———➤●◄———

TWO LITTLE MICE WHO WERE LIVING in the city decided to go out on the town. He waited for her at the corner of Cheese St. and Trapp Rd. They were not allowed to show themselves because the people would freak. The light turned green for them to proceed and they mingled among the people's feet and no one ever saw them. They couldn't get on the side walk from the road so they had to use the ramp. It's a good thing no one saw them, they may have been trampled. They ran straight for the wall of the building to rest for a few minutes and to catch their breath.

Lucy asked Jake "Where are we going?"

"Down to the restaurant to have some fun." Jake said.

"I'm not going with you because we are not allowed in those places."

As they ran down the street dodging in out of peoples foot steps they were out of breath for the second time.

"I don't know about you but I haven't had any fun yet. How do we get in?"

"Stick with me kid and I will show you."

They finally reached the door of the restaurant.

"Give me your hand. When someone opens the door to go

in or out that's when we will pass through." Jake said.

"Then what?"

"Follow me. Keep out of sight, run along the wall, under the tables then out where they cook the food. You didn't know we would be going out for dinner to such a posh place to eat when I asked you for a date."

The evening went smooth; they had a good supper of pheasant under glass with all the trimmings. After they had eaten they both laid on the floor rubbing their little bellies because they had over eaten.

"We have to leave this place the same way we got in."

They finally left and on their way home he asked her if she had a good time.

"Oh yes. I have never seen so many feet in my whole life and all going in different directions."

They laughed all the way home.

"Shall we do it again next week?"

"I don't know," said Lucy, "It will take me all week to get over this excitement. If we do go out next week lets go somewhere else since it is my birthday."

"Okay." said Jake.

Next week came and they met at the same place and were happy to see each other.

"Where are you taking me this time?" asked Lucy.

"Oh, we are going down to the race track and bet on some horses."

However when they arrived at the stables where the horses were kept they ran around the horses feet and scared them and they were dancing on all fours. They left then and went back to the restaurant where they had been the week before. When it was time to leave Jake said,

"I'll walk you home.

"Okay." said Lucy, "I live down here in a hole in the wall.

When we get there you'll see some really huge cats that live in the alley."

They had an exciting evening and vowed to do it again real soon.

Jake thought for a moment then said, "Lucy, you should find another hole in the wall to live where the cats aren't so large."

"I'll see." she said, "Why Jake, are you afraid of the cats?" as she smiled at him showing her sharp little teeth and little pink lips.

Printed in the United States
by Baker & Taylor Publisher Services